THE LAW OF ATTRACTION FOR...

SALES

J.M. Edwards

HOW TO CONNECT THE DOTS TO GET WHAT YOU WANT

FIRST EDITION

Published in the United States of America by
InterSkillMedia Publishing. Round Rock, Texas 78681

All rights reserved. No part of this book may be reproduced, copied, stored, or transmitted in any form or by any means graphic, electronic, or mechanical, including photocopying, recording, or information storage and retrieval systems without the prior written permission of InterSkillMedia, except where permitted by law.

'The Law of Attraction For...' is the sole trademark of InterSkillMedia.

Copyright, 2009 by InterSkillMedia

To purchase other titles or to purchase the audio version of this title, please visit, www.InterSkillMedia.com

ISBN 10: 0-9820797-6-1

ISBN 13: 978-0-9820797-6-8

Made in The United States of America.

May, 2009

www.InterSkillMedia.com

Book Cover Design By Austen Heath

Contents

Preface

1. **What Is The Law of Attraction?**
2. **What Is Your Goal?**
3. **Belief Makes It Happen**
4. **Visualization**
5. **The Role of Persistence**
6. **The Positive Mind**
7. **Gratitude**
8. **The Cues of Influence**
9. **The Power of Likeability**
10. **It's All About Feelings**
11. **Body Language**
12. **Obstacles**
13. **Respecting Individuality**
14. **Emotional Payoffs**
15. **The Value of Questions**
16. **Assume The Sale**
17. **Monetize The Benefits**
18. **Stop Talking!**
19. **Pick Your Company**
20. **Living The Law of Attraction**

Preface

The Law of Attraction is not new. The ideas and concepts have been around for a very long time. What is new and different is the extraordinary amount of current interest on the subject. More than ever before, people are more than curious to know about The Law of Attraction and, for good reason.

Each and every one of us wants our hopes and dreams to come true. The challenge is - knowing how to go about getting what we really want.

Other than lottery winners who rely on chance, many individuals achieve success through hard work and sheer determination. We live, though, among a generation where patience and hard work are not necessarily admired. We also live in an instant generation where new technology has created a, 'get what you want now rather than later mind-set'.

After reading one or more popular books on the subject, many followers of its principles feel The Law of Attraction will provide easy money and guaranteed success. That is not realistic thinking.

The Law of Attraction is real and it is powerful when understood and used correctly. What you must recognize is the fact that simply wanting something will not change the order of the universe and therefore hand it over to you on a silver platter. Truthfully, there are many things that can get in the way of your success that The Law of Attraction will not solve. For example, if a person chooses to follow The Law of Attraction and its principles and ultimately wants to become successful in Sales yet, is pessimistic by nature, has poor hygiene, does not listen to customers or is unable to decode a customer's body language, then success in Sales is very unlikely to happen.

This book was designed to help you connect the dots between each component of successful selling and using The Law of Attraction and its timeless principles in your career to get what you want. To be successful in Sales, there must be a balance between using The Law of Attraction principles and setting realistic and achievable goals, knowing the most effective ways in which to influence customer behavior and, how to make the most of your Sales presentations by encoding and decoding body language with each and every customer interaction. I call this process, 'connecting the dots'.

Have you ever played the game where you connect the dots on a page and when all the dots were finally connected, low and behold, all the dots together created an image that you did not see at first? But, after connecting all the dots, the entire picture was clear as a horse, a car or perhaps a person appeared. However, if all the dots were not connected, isn't it obvious that the image would be incomplete. Of course! That is why The Law of Attraction will not, in and of itself, make you successful.

To achieve personal success in Sales, all of the dots must be connected. Even if you are intrigued by The Law of Attraction and the amazing power and influence it can have upon your potential success but, you do not believe in yourself, you are unlikely to ever realize the level of success you are actually capable of achieving. The entire process of Sales can be compared to a long chain. Each aspect of Sales is similar to each link in the chain. For example, dress and grooming would be one link. How to artfully ask questions would be another. When all the links are connected together, the chain becomes very strong.

The Law of Attraction pulls the chain. It is like the engine in an automobile. The engine gives forth horsepower and is the driving force that makes the automobile a reality. The windshield, tires, steering wheel and transmission are all components that the automobile must have in order to operate successfully.

The Law of Attraction For..Sales can help you connect the dots to create a successful future for yourself. Not only will you be able to connect the dots, you will be able to establish very strong links in the Sales chain. And, once your chain of success is in place, The Law of Attraction will be the driving force to get you where you want to go.

In this book, you will learn how to use The Law of Attraction to create unlimited success as well as the necessary links that can make all your goals not only a dream but, a reality.

It is an exciting journey. The only limit is your imagination. So, buckle up and hang on. You're about to go on a ride of a lifetime!

One
What Is The Law of Attraction?

Research indicates that the first real mention of the actual term "Law of Attraction" other than Hinduism, is in a book on esoteric mysteries, written by Helena Blavatsky, in 1877.

The New York Times, in 1879, was the first major newspaper to use the phrase "Law of Attraction". The newspaper described the wagon trains of the Colorado gold rush as "moving in obedience to some occult law of attraction that overcomes all obstacles in their progress to their destination".

In the early 1900s, Thomas Troward, who was a strong influence in the New Thought Movement, claimed that thought precedes physical form and that "the action of mind plants that nucleus which, if allowed to grow undisturbed, will eventually attract to itself all the conditions necessary for its manifestation in outward visible form".

In 1912, Charles Haanel, author of The Master Key System described The Law of Attraction as "the greatest and most infallible law upon which the entire system of creation depends."

Just six years earlier, in 1906, William Walker Atkinson described The Law of Attraction in his book, *Thought Vibration, or The Law of Attraction in the Thought World*. In this early twentieth century book of enlightenment, Atkinson wrote: "We speak learnedly of the Law of Gravitation, but ignore that equally wonderful manifestation, THE LAW OF ATTRACTION IN THE THOUGHT WORLD. We are familiar with that wonderful manifestation of Law which draws us and holds together the atoms of which matter is composed – we recognize the power of the law that attracts bodies to the earth, that holds the circling worlds in their places, but we close our eyes to the *mighty law that draws to us the things we desire or fear, that makes or mars our fears.* When we come to see that Thought is a force – a manifestation of energy – having a magnet-like power of attraction, we will begin to understand the why and the wherefore of many things that have heretofore seemed dark to us. There is no study that will so well repay the student for his time and trouble as the study of the workings of this mighty law of the world of Thought – The Law of Attraction".

William Atkinson saw The Law of Attraction as important and as meaningful as The Law of Gravity. He said that "we speak learnedly" but ignore that equally wonderful manifestation THE LAW OF ATTRACTION IN THE THOUGHT WORLD.

He recognized that the majority of humanity had ignored the mighty Law of Attraction that draws to us the things we desire and fear.

People around the entire globe experience The Law of Attraction. Most have no clue that the life they are constantly creating for themselves is due to this universal law. To learn what The Law of Attraction is and how it is best defined, let's first examine a few quotes from individuals who understood and lived its principles.

"You create your own universe as you go along" – Winston Churchill

"If you think you can you probably will, if you think you can't, you're right" – Henry Ford

"Imagination is everything. It is the preview of life's coming attractions" – Albert Einstein

"I will see it when I believe it" – Wayne Dyer

"Follow your bliss, and doors will open for you that you never knew existed" – Joseph Campbell

"Let a person radically alter his thoughts, and he will be astonished at the rapid transformation it will effect in the material conditions of his life" – James Allen

"Take the first step in faith. You don't have to see the whole staircase, just take the first step" – Martin Luther King Jr.

"**What you resist persists**" – Carl Jung

"I am no longer cursed by poverty because I took possession of my own mind, and that mind has yielded me every material thing I want, and much more than I need. But, this power of mind is a universal one, available to the humblest person as it is to the greatest" – Andrew Carnegie

"Whatever your mind can conceive and can believe, it can achieve" – Napoleon Hill

You should now have a better understanding of what The Law of Attraction is. However, let's dig deeper to learn, not only how The Law of Attraction affects us individually but, how it works and, more importantly, how to create for yourself the very best life possible using this powerful universal law.

First, take a moment to examine your life right now. You can better understand The Law of Attraction if you take time to reflect upon the life you have right now, at this very moment. You see, the house you live in, the car you drive, the type of clothes you wear, the job or career you have, your friends, the amount of money you have or don't have are all a direct result of The Law of Attraction.

The Law of Attraction is summed up in just one sentence, 'you are what you continually think about and focus upon'.

The life you are living right now is the sum total of your past thoughts. In other words, your present existence is the accumulation of your prior thoughts. What you have been thinking about and focusing upon the past five, ten or even twenty years has brought you to where you are today and the life you now experience.

Let's go back to Napoleon Hill's words.

"Whatever your mind can conceive and can believe, it can achieve".

Before we move on, you must understand that The Law of Attraction begins and ends with your mind. If you take control of your thoughts, you can then control your life, bringing your hopes and dreams into reality.

Like Attracts Like

The Law of Attraction dictates that like thoughts attract more of the same. The primary principle of The Law of Attraction states that 'like attracts like'. Whatever you focus on, that is what you experience or bring into your life. If you continue to focus on not having enough money then, you will never have enough money. If, on the other hand, you think about and focus on having plenty of money then, you will have, as Andrew Carnegie stated, more money than you will ever need.

It is the mind that The Law of Attraction originates. Your mind is very powerful. The Law of Attraction is the most loyal servant you could ever want in that it brings to you whatever you command. If, in your mind, you focus on a particular thing, the universal Law of Attraction will attract it to you.

Your Thoughts Have Power

Like everyone, you have hopes and dreams of the future. Bringing those hopes and dreams to reality begins with your thoughts and, more importantly, what you continually think about. Time and again this cycle occurs many times over. A person begins with nothing. Dreams about and focuses on prosperity. Works hard to accumulate wealth and possessions and achieves those hopes and dreams. Next, he or she worries and continually thinks about losing the wealth and possessions they have acquired only to lose it all. Then, he or she starts over with nothing and focuses upon and thinks only about accumulating wealth and possessions. And, finally achieves wealth and possessions again.

In this example, you saw someone with nothing achieve their dreams only to lose everything. Then, after losing it all, they reacquired wealth and possessions after their fear of loss was replaced by thoughts of acquiring new wealth. The Law of Attraction responds to your thoughts. Again, like attracts like. Your thoughts become a reality.

Imagine for a moment that your thoughts are like a large magnet. Your thoughts attract to you what you are predominately thinking about.

If you constantly complain about your health or how bad you feel, you attract similar thoughts until you feel even worse. If you complain about how much money you don't have, you attract more and more of the same.

Andrew Carnegie stated that he took control of his mind. That is the beginning of your success and enjoying the life you desire. Take control. Become aware of your dominant thoughts. Become aware of the pattern of your thinking. Until you continually focus on what you do want rather than want you do not want, you will receive more of the same and your life will never change.

Your Dominant Thoughts

Your dominant thoughts can be described as your pattern of thoughts. These patterns are typically divided into positive and negative thoughts.

If you focus upon what you do want then, your thoughts are more positive. If, on the other hand, your thoughts are focused upon what you do not want, they tend to be negative. Focusing on your hopes and dreams for the future, the things that you do want, is a positive experience while focusing on what you do not want in a pessimistic way creates a negative experience or environment, especially for the people around you.

The Law of Attraction is interpreted by many as attracting money or wealth. But, equal consideration must be given to the avoidance of attracting what you do not want through negative thought patterns.

Winston Churchill and Joe McCarthy

These two men illustrate the difference between positive versus negative dominant thought patterns. While both men were politicians, the focus here is not a political one but, a study in human behavior and examining positive and negative thought patterns.

"The pessimist sees the difficulty in every opportunity; an optimist sees the opportunity in every difficulty".

"Courage is going from failure to failure without losing enthusiasm".

"Success is not final, failure is not fatal: it is the courage to continue that counts".

"Attitude is a little thing that makes a big difference".

"If you are going through hell, keep going".

Winston Churchill (1874 – 1965) is attributed to those words. While they are interesting quotes, they reveal the statesman's dominant thought patterns. His dominant thought patterns were continually positive. It was Winston Churchill who also said: "Never give in, never give in, never; never; never; never – in nothing great or small, large or petty – never give in except to convictions of honor and good sense".

His dominant thought patterns were continually positive as he focused on the future as his legacy confirms. Churchill lived through one of the most difficult periods in mankind's history, World War II. His dominant thought patterns focused on what he wanted and attracted more of the same, revealing determination and courage in the face of an evil dictator, Adolf Hitler.

Churchill lived into his 90th year.

Conversely, Joe McCarthy (1908 – 1957) is the Senator who investigated communism during the 1950's. His words and actions reveal a dominant negative thought pattern. Whether his tactics were justified is not the point here. His negative thought patterns attracted more of the same which created an environment that eventually cost him his political career. He suffered from alcoholism and died from acute hepatitis.

McCarthy died at the age of 48.

There Is Nothing You Can't Accomplish

Addressing a joint session of Congress on May 25, 1961, President John F Kennedy stated:

"First, I believe that this nation should commit itself to achieving the goal, before this decade is out, of landing a man on the Moon and returning him back safely to the earth. No single space project in this period will be more impressive to mankind or more important for the long-range exploration of space; and none will be so difficult or expensive to accomplish."

True to the President's words, the goal of landing a man on the Moon by the end of the decade was accomplished. The United States space agency NASA achieved the first manned landing on Earth's Moon as part of the Apollo 11 mission commanded by Neil Armstrong. On July 20, 1969, Armstrong landed the lunar module *Eagle* on the surface of the Moon with a companion, while the third astronaut orbited above.

What does this accomplishment teach us?

It helps us to understand that anything we desire can be accomplished. Even if you do not have the resources, The Law of Attraction and your continued focus and attention on what you do want will attract those resources to you.

A great many books have been written about The Law of Attraction in just the past few years. The information contained in those books has helped millions to better understand and utilize the benefits of The Law of Attraction.

The following is a list of titles that will help you better understand the principles of The Law of Attraction:

"Think & Grow Rich" by Napoleon Hill

"You Can If You Think You Can" by Norman Vincent Peale.

"The Secret" by Rhonda Byrne

"The Law of Attraction" by Esther and Jerry Hicks

"The Key" by Joe Vitale

"The Law of Attraction: The Science of Attracting More of What You Want and Less of What You Don't" by Michael J. Losier.

"The Law of Attraction in Action: A Down-to-Earth Guide to Transforming Your Life (No Matter Where You're Starting From)" by Deanna Davis, PhD   .

The challenge everyone faces when attempting to bring The Law of Attraction into their lives is overcoming the obstacles that oppose you and hinder you from achieving your hopes and dreams, whatever they are. The books just mentioned are invaluable tools in that respect.

This book is not designed to talk about this mighty law alone, but to help you to achieve your goals when other things can and will get in the way. This book is dedicated to the practical application of The Law of Attraction as it applies to a career in Sales.

This book also focuses on the all important, 'How To'. While most of the books on the subject deliver an excellent understanding of The Law of Attraction, it is the practical components of Sales, the negative thought patterns, external and internal, that get in the way that this book considers.

Finally, this book addresses the obstacles and challenges to become successful in Sales and how to overcome them.

It also focuses on the most important strategies that can help you fully benefit from this mighty law, The Law of Attraction.

*A deeply entrenched goal
will become a reality*

Two
What Is Your Goal?

To achieve success, you must have a clear and specific goal in mind and let nothing stop you from obtaining it.

Imagine a gladiator who enters the arena without a clear objective. The likelihood of his survival is not only doubtful, it is absolutely impossible.

This comparison should strike you as being completely ridiculous. Why would the gladiator step into the arena without knowing what he was there for in the first place?

He would have to be mentally challenged not knowing what his specific purpose or goal was prior to making such a life threatening decision. Likewise, would it not also be ridiculous for someone to attempt to be successful in a competitive Sales environment and not have a clear objective or goal in mind?

Every day, Salespeople follow in the footsteps of the mentally challenged gladiator getting killed by their competitors. Completely unaware as to why they were beaten in the first place.

Most industries today are highly competitive. Survival requires extreme commitment that involves goal setting to achieve extraordinary results. In Sales, you will not survive if you are just an *average* Salesperson. An average Salesperson can be described an one who never attempts to exceed customer expectations, is not concerned with his or her appearance, is satisfied with an average income and usually slacks off toward the end of the month when all the necessary bills have been paid and a little extra money is in the bank.

Average Salespeople are fearful of setting goals.

While there are many reasons why a Salesperson would not make goal setting a primary focus, most of the time the average Salesperson is simply comfortable with the status quo.

Setting goals requires measured and controlled thought accompanied by energy, determination and commitment necessary to achieve a specific objective. The average Salesperson lacks sufficient knowledge and the understanding of the power of goal setting and its countless benefits.

If you are serious about The Law of Attraction and the achievement of all your hopes and dreams, then let's discuss the power and the benefits of goal setting, starting with the first benefit - Control.

Setting goals give you a sense of direction and more importantly, a sense of control.

The Role of Control

Life satisfaction is closely tied to the degree of control one feels they have at any given moment.

Imagine sitting in the back seat of a four-door sedan careening down a steep highway. Now, picture the driver.

Sixteen years old and today is their first day with a license to drive. Worse, the young teen has no experience driving down a steep mountain. How safe do you feel in the back seat? Can you feel the anxiety and lack of control?

The anxiety you feel is a result of your lack of control. If you were the driver, obviously your anxiety would be much lower as you feel you have more control of the vehicle going down the steep mountain.

In Sales, your anxiety level is linked to the degree of control you have over your Sales and more importantly, your income. Lose a customer and a portion of your income and you will feel a degree of anxiety. This is due to the perceived loss of control as you are no longer behind the wheel.

Setting a goal and striving to achieve it, not only gives you a sense of direction, it gives you a sense of control. A state of mind that allows you to make good decisions that ultimately will affect your success.

Goal Mapping

The part of the process that is most enjoyable is taking the time to sit down and envision your goal. You should ask yourself, what is it that I want?

Let your mind go free and explore your inner most desires.

Do not stop at a certain annual income. Think about how that amount of income would change your lifestyle. Where would you live? What kind of house, condo or apartment would you live in? What car or vehicle would you drive? Imagine the clothes you would wear. New friends you would meet, and so on.

This step is vital. If you are to achieve anything worthwhile, you must conclude on your own, what it is that you really want. For you to strive hard to achieve success or have the energy to keep moving forward, you must have a clear picture in your mind of what your goal is and why you want it.

Define Your Goal

Identifying your very own specific goal is the first link in your success chain. In Sales, many people plug along each day without a specific goal in mind. They accomplish little because they fail to dream more than what they have or set a specific goal as to what they really want. They stumble along with nothing clearly defined as to what they must do to get where they want to go.

Master sales trainer and best-selling author, Zig Ziglar is credited for stating;

'You can't hit a target that you cannot see'.

To succeed in Sales, you must have a clear vision of what it is that you really want to accomplish.

Do you want to be the top Salesperson in your company or organization? Do you want to earn a six figure annual income? Do you want to become debt free? Do you need a specific amount of money to pay off college loans or retire?

The word goal literally means 'the end toward which effort is directed'. To get what you want for yourself and your family, you must decide what you want or establish your very own 'end'.

Your goal.

In modern day sports, the end is called 'home plate' or even better, the 'end zone'.

To some, deciding what they really want can be painfully difficult. What do you really want? What are you willing to sacrifice to create a better future for yourself?

The best way to identify what you really want is to make a list of what you envision your future to be like. Once you have a list, rate them all on a scale of one to ten with one being the least and ten being the most important goal. This will help you to sort out what is most important to you.

Then, once you have established what you want in detail, set a *time limit* to accomplish it.

A Time Limit

A time limit will help you stay focused on the 'end'. Whatever goal you choose, the common denominator is a number, either in dollars or perhaps units of Sales.

In each case, you will be targeting a number to reach. Measuring yourself is the primary means in which to achieve your goal. With measurement, you can track your progress and make adjustments as you go.

Let's say you want to make a certain amount of money per month. $10,000, for example. It is not enough to simply dream about making $10,000 per month. Dreaming is fun but, it is just the beginning. Now that we have a specific goal, $10,000, we now have a time limit. $10,000 per month. Since there are typically four weeks in a month, we can divide $10,000 by four and now have a weekly goal that will match your monthly goal. $2,500 per week.

However, we also need to go one step further. We also need a daily goal. Therefore, since there are approximately twenty business days in a month, the daily goal should be $500.

By breaking down your goal into increments such as day and month, you are much more likely to focus on your goal on a consistent basis. Waiting to the end of the month to give serious attention to your monthly goal is a formula for failure.

Write It Down

It is one thing to imagine your goal. It is another to achieve it without writing your specific goal down where you can see it daily.

Leaving your goal alone in your mind will cause your goal to fade away. Eventually, the goal will disappear as your mind has many other things to think about. Like an airport, your thoughts are like passengers who come and go from one destination to another. Without constant attention, your goal will fly away to another destination and never return.

Have you ever noticed how fast a home can deteriorate when no one occupies it? Weeds start to take over. The shingles start to fall off. The paint starts to peel.

Think about a garden for a moment. A garden takes constant care. Miss a day or two or worse, a week and, then look at your garden. What do you find? It is nothing but weeds. Soon, your garden will become a jungle.

Your mind works much the same way. When you think about what you want at first and then miss a day or two without thinking about it or you have stopped altogether, your goal will hide in the far corners of your mind. Eventually, it will fade away and your goal will be lost and never become a reality.

A powerful thing the mind is. Think about something every day and your mind becomes a construction site building a mental highway to a specific destination - your goal you have envisioned.

Write it down where you can see it every morning when you wake up or before you go to bed at night. This will help you to stay focused on your goal and not be distracted with the anxieties of life.

Every time you think about your goal, your mind goes to work to make it a reality. Writing your goal down and thereafter mentally reviewing it every day will help your goal become part of your future.

This is where The Law of Attraction takes over. As you have your goal constantly in mind, opportunities will appear as your mind attracts things that will help to make your goal a reality.

But, do not stop there. Additionally, write your goal on the back of your business card or a small index card and keep it in your pocket at all times when you are working. You will forget about your goal during the day as you have many things to do. However, as you put your hand in your pocket during the day, you will feel the card and your goal will flash back into your mind. Therefore, keeping your dream constantly before you is how your goal lives on.

The Law of Attraction is a matter of staying focused. What you *consistently* think about becomes your reality. The ability to stay focused on your goal by using these techniques puts The Law of Attraction in action.

Track Your Goal

To stay on point with your goal, it is wise to decide how you will keep track of your goal. Many use a spreadsheet to measure their progress. It really doesn't matter how you keep track. What matters is that you stay consistent with your own method of tracking your progress.

If you decide to change the method of how you keep track, wait until the end of a month to do so. The last thing you want is to miss recording your progress for only a day. This could cause you to stop altogether.

Remember to stay consistent.

This is where the magic starts to happen!

A goal gives you a sense of direction and control

When you track your daily, weekly and monthly progress toward your goal, you will notice how your decision making will be affected by your progress or lack thereof.

It is as if your measuring is a silent partner or perhaps an inner voice urging you to press on.

Nothing happens without measurement. Think of how many things are accomplished due to measuring. Cooking, building a house or even passing an exam at school involves measuring. Few things are accomplished on a consistent basis without it.

Short Term vs Long Term

Goals are broken down into two categories. Short Term and Long Term. Which one should you focus on first? It's an appropriate question. Deciding what you will tackle each day can and will determine the degree of success you will eventually realize.

Let's go back to the sub-heading, *Define Your Goal*. Here, the definition of the word goal was revealed. The word, 'goal' literally means, "the end toward which effort is directed."

Start with the 'end' and then work backward. Start with your long term goal and then work back until you have decided the actions you will take in the next twenty-four hours. For example, under the sub-heading, *A Time Limit*, the 'end' or goal was to make $10,000 per month. That could be your long term goal. Working back, the discovery was made that one would need to generate $500 per day to achieve the long term goal of making $10,000 per month. That is how 'working backward' can help you to achieve your goal.

Now that we know what our Short Term goal is. $500 per day. We can now decide what steps we need to take today to achieve the Long Term goal of $10,000 per month.

The Law of Attraction can and will have a dramatic impact upon your goals. However, even though The Law of Attraction will help bring people, circumstances and events to your attention as opportunities, you must have a plan and thereafter, you must work your plan until you have successfully accomplished your goal.

The Law of Attraction in Action!

The Law of Attraction is never a means to an end. However, your goals are. Setting your goals allows The Law of Attraction to work in your favor.

Remember, your thoughts become things. With your thoughts, you attract what it is that you do want and you also attract what it is that you do not want. Whether you are tuned into The Law of Attraction or not, it is at work within you right now, the last twenty-four hours, last year and so on. What you have in your life, the type of car that you drive, the house or apartment that you live in and even your career, all of these things are a reality of your historical thoughts.

The way in which you think creates your life and everything that is in it. If you continue to tell yourself,

"I'll never be able to make this happen". You are correct. It will never happen. If you listen to others who tell you that you should not attempt to achieve your goals for fear of failure, you must reject those thoughts immediately and never allow them to enter your mind again.

On the other hand, if you focus on your goal and continue to tell yourself that you can make it happen and you visualize in your mind having already achieved your goal, then your goal can become a reality.

It will become the manifestation of your thoughts.

Goals Create Energy

When a desirable goal has been set, something remarkable takes place. A goal creates energy. Every day, people accomplish extraordinary things because they established a goal that was intensely desirable. To accomplish anything worthwhile requires effort. When you set a goal that is desirable, energy from within you becomes the driving force.

Plan vs Purpose

Many fail to achieve their goals because set-backs were experienced or things just didn't go according to 'plan'. This is where understanding the difference between planning and purpose comes in. Once you have set your goal and begin to work backward to create a plan of action for each month, each week and each day, you must realize that unforeseen events will occur. You just do not have complete control over events that will set you back. Therefore, you must be prepared to *adjust* your plan.

The word purpose means, 'something set up as an object or end to be attained'. Having your purpose or goal clearly defined allows you to make adjustments along the way.

This will keep you from becoming discouraged when something happens that did not go the way you had planned. You must accept that something will happen that will be unexpected. Many times, however, what appears to be a set-back is actually an opportunity.

The Law of Attraction creates opportunities.

Because you have full belief that what you have set as a goal will happen, The Law of Attraction will present opportunities along the way that will help make your goal a reality.

Dream Big

Your dreams are only limited by your imagination and what you truly desire. As stated in the previous chapter, putting a man on the moon demonstrates that there is nothing you can't have or accomplish. Let's see how that goal originated and, thereafter accomplished.

On May 25, 1961, President John F. Kennedy presented an extraordinary goal to the Congress of the United States. He called for a mission to send a man to the moon. He said, "I believe that this nation should commit itself to achieving the goal, before this decade is out, of landing a man on the moon and returning him safely to the Earth."

Some thought that his declaration was lunacy. Sending a man to the moon seemed not only daunting, it would be costly. And, it was. The president cautioned the Congress that the cost would be very high, more than $9 billion in 1960s dollars. "No single space project in this period will be more impressive to mankind or more important for the long-range exploration of space; and none will be so difficult or expensive to accomplish", Kennedy said.

Congress, however, accepted the challenge and history was made. Without a clearly defined goal, the concept of sending a man to the moon would not have been possible. However, feeling a sense of urgency in finding a way to overtake the Soviets in the space race, Kennedy had met with Vice President Lyndon Johnson and his science advisers to come up with a plan to accomplish such an extraordinary historical goal.

Despite severe skepticism from those who thought it could not be accomplished, Kennedy's dream became a reality on July 20, 1969, when Apollo 11 commander Neil Armstrong landed on the moon and safely returned to earth. The goal was accomplished and within the time limit. Without the audacity to dream, nothing extraordinary takes pace.

Your future will be made with or without you.

Decide for yourself that now is the time to set short term as well as long term goals. Your future is in your hands. Choose not to be discouraged when set-backs occur but, continue to press on.

*Faith is an assured expectation of reality
though not presently beheld*

Three
Belief Makes It Happen

The speed in which you accomplish your goals will be determined by the degree in which you believe in yourself.

When you express belief, the second link in the chain of success, you are accepting something to be true or real. To believe you can create success means that you already see yourself as being successful. It is not just a matter of dreaming or visualizing what you want to create for yourself, it is the intensity of your conviction.

Belief can be optimistic or pessimistic. It can either move you toward your goal or keep success at bay. Nevertheless, it all starts with the conversations that take place inside your head. These conversations are often called self-talk or inner dialogue. No matter the label that is placed upon them, these mental conversations will dramatically shape your subconscious beliefs. They are very powerful because they direct your decision making and shape your belief system. In these conversations, we explain to ourselves why good events take place and subsequently, why bad events happen.

Optimistic or pessimistic, it is simply a matter of which one you predominantly listen to that will ultimately shape your beliefs.

The Power of Your Thoughts

The power of belief begins with the mind. To create success, you must understand how the mind plays a key role in the journey toward success. Within your mind are negative and positive thought patterns. Ultimately, you will choose which thought patterns dominate your thinking. Each thought pattern can be compared to two best friends with very different opinions. These two friends are good at listening to your hopes and dreams then afterward share their deep seated opinions with you. They care for you and are absolutely obedient in anything you ask them to do.

Let's imagine that you want to start a new job in commission Sales and you seek out the opinion of your two best friends. One is always supportive and positive while the other is the complete opposite. This particular friend is extremely fearful of Sales. Before you make your decision to go on your first interview for a position in commission Sales, you sit down with the friend who is pessimistic.

In the comfort of your living room, you begin to tell her what you have planned. You know this particular friend is usually cautious and not at all positive but, you listen anyway. You have no reason to distrust her opinion, as she has always had your best interest at heart. After listening to your explanation as to what you have in mind and, because you have opened the door to her influence, she is generous in helping you to recall similar experiences that would help confirm that commission Sales would be a disaster.

This particular friend reminds you of the relative who tried commission Sales once and not only did it not work out, the loss of income severely set the person back financially.

They had to move to a less expensive apartment and their credit was damaged as they were not able to pay their bills on time.

After she is finished, your dream begins to fade. At this point you have no energy left. What once was an enthusiastic proposition now is a dangerous one. But, before your best friend leaves, she feels, in her educated opinion, that you need help in recalling more bad events. Therefore, she brings to your attention numerous unsuccessful attempts you or anyone else has ever made toward success in Sales. Like a museum, she takes you to a room full of exhibits where each and every set-back she holds in her memory for you is on display. As you stand looking at all the exhibits, you notice that each memory is written in stone and lies beneath a glass case. Each memory on display seems to reaffirm what the overly cautious best friend had already shared with you. In the first exhibit, well lit with a gold frame, is the well preserved memory of the first time you ever tried Sales. It had been a complete failure. Each time you are reminded or think about this particular bad event, its memory and all the details surrounding the event are preserved, as if placed in a museum exhibit.

In the next exhibit, the memory of another friend is well preserved. This friend was formerly in Sales but, lost their job because they could not make the monthly quota. As you relive the details of each memory you are, in effect, symbolically dusting off the glass case of each exhibit helping to further preserve each memory.

Finally, after you have seen all the exhibits in the museum, your worst fears have been confirmed. Sales would be much too dangerous and the risk would not be worth the effort.

The question now is, what will you do? Listen to the best friend who has strongly encouraged you to avoid such an undertaking and to forget the idea of getting started in commission Sales or, will you argue against these negative thoughts?

Argue Against Reality

Unlike the best friend who lives next door, this particular friend lives across town and quickly and enthusiastically comes over whenever she is called upon. In the past, she has also proven to be positive and supportive.

After explaining the opportunity for more income with commission Sales and the negative thoughts the cautious best friend previously shared, the supportive friend goes to work. What does she do? She argues against reality. What does this mean? The reality is that there are no guarantees that you will be absolutely successful in commission Sales. The reality is that your income, in the beginning, may be less than what you had hoped for. The reality is that many Salespeople come and go when attempting to venture into commission Sales and some leave, never to return. These are all very real possibilities. Collectively, they make up the realities of commission Sales.

In arguing against reality, the supportive best friend explains that even though there are no absolute guarantees in commission Sales, the evidence is there to give commission Sales a try. She argues that in your previous attempts you did not have the opportunity to be trained before getting started. This is something that you remember quite well. She also reminds you of the fact that the friend who lost their job for not making the required quota had shown very little initiative to even try to meet the quota. You even remember her saying that the friend did not really like commission Sales in the first place. And, the supportive best friend reminds you of your talents and skills when it comes to communicating. She reminds you of your ability to influence others to make a decision and especially when the customer will greatly benefit. She also reminds you of your excellent people skills and warm personality that, according to her, would definitely help you to succeed in Sales.

Finally, she brings to your attention that not only can you sell anything that you whole heartedly believe in, she helps you to recall how competitive you are and your innermost desire to improve your lifestyle.

Interestingly, we argue against reality every day without even thinking about it. For example, every year in the United States more than 40,000 people die in auto accidents. That is a reality. We cannot listen to the television news or read the local newspaper without learning that someone has died in an auto accident. But, we continue to drive nonetheless. Why? It is because we continue to argue against reality. When we hear such heartbreaking news, we explain to ourselves why it is not likely to happen to us. We rationalize that the number of fatal auto accidents as compared to the number of drivers on the road are very low. We also reason that we are a careful driver. We wear a seat belt at all times and so on. Yes, every single day we argue against reality.

Not driving an automobile is a significant inconvenience. This fact, coupled with the desire to have the freedom to drive allows each of us the ability to control any fear we may have about dying in an auto accident. Our ability to argue against reality enables us to drive our vehicles without fear or apprehension.

In each of our minds, these two best friends exist. Once they have been summoned, they are both ready to come to our aid with very strong opinions that will ultimately affect the way in which we make up our minds about our own future.

The cautious best friend indeed lives next door. This means it is easier for you to immediately think negative thoughts than to ponder positive thoughts that enable you to argue against reality. Conversely, the best friend who lives across town means that effort will need to be expended to hear supportive and positive reinforcement in order to argue against negative thinking or the realities of life.

The good news is that we are the ones that control whether or not we will listen to negative or positive self-talk that will help us to make our own decisions.

In addition, we usually hear either negative or positive comments from family or friends who weigh in on our hopes and dreams. In any event, we have the choice at all times to argue against reality. But, never should you surrender your dreams or your future simply because someone has introduced negative thinking. Do not give up. These are your dreams and not theirs. Even with good intentions, many times family and friends offer negative comments due to their own past failures. It is not the fact that they do not want you to succeed. They are usually trying to keep you from suffering when your goals do not materialize. Keep in mind, however, that this is your future and it is yours to decide.

This does not mean, of course, that you should throw caution to the wind. You should weigh the pros and cons of any decision. You should seek out the counsel of those you trust and those who have experience before embarking upon a new adventure. Use their input to help you make a wise and well informed decision.

Believe You Can and You Will

The Law of Attraction will help you achieve what you desire when intense belief is present. Positive thoughts attract more positive thoughts.

When you fully believe that you will succeed, you will see doors of opportunity open to you that will lead you to your goal. Without intense belief and a positive mental attitude, you will not see these doors of opportunity. Remember, like attracts like.

Intense belief keeps doubt from entering your mind.

Unwavering belief in yourself and your goals gives you the energy to keep going. As each day passes by, you will see these doors of opportunity opening to you. It will seem that opportunities are moving toward you and they are, however, these opportunities become visible because your mind is attracting them as you move toward your goal.

The Law of Attraction is at work when purchasing a new vehicle. When you purchase a new vehicle, you possess a very positive frame of mind. You're happy and content that you've made the purchase of a new vehicle. You feel many positive emotions. Now, as you drive around, you begin to notice other vehicles just like the one you drove home from the dealership. Same make, same model. As days turn into weeks, it seems that almost everyone is now driving the same vehicle that you are. How is it that you never noticed them before? Obviously, you didn't buy the very first vehicle of its kind.

When you have absolute belief that your desires will become a reality along with a positive mental attitude, doors of opportunity will open up for you. If you have set a clearly defined goal then, you will see each door. If, however, you are not in a positive frame of mind and you have no clear goal in which you are trying to achieve, then the door will not be visible to you.

It will be the same as with the purchase of the new vehicle. Before you made the purchase, you never really saw that many vehicles on the road of the same type. It is as if they were invisible. Now that you have that same vehicle you see them. This is The Law of Attraction at work.

The stronger you belief in yourself and what you want to achieve, each decision you make will help you toward success. If, for example, you set a goal to have six months of income in a savings or mutual fund account and you have set a time limit to achieve the goal then, each and every decision you make will be affected by that goal. If you believe that you will achieve your goal within the time limit, your absolute belief in your goal will give you the self discipline to turn down unnecessary purchases that would prevent you from achieving your goal. Your absolute belief will attract opportunities to earn additional income that will help you to meet your objective.

This is where your chain of success comes in. If you do not have an intense desire or an absolute belief that you can achieve your goal, then doubt will cause this most important link, that of 'belief', to weaken when The Law of Attraction presents a door of opportunity.

Here is an example, let's imagine your past monthly income has been $5,000 per month and you desire six months of income or $30,000 put away in the event of an emergency or an accident that might keep you from working for a period of time. But, doubt enters your mind as to the unlikelihood of your ability to achieve the goal and you say to yourself, "There is no way I can save $30,000. Even if I put aside $500 per month it will take me five years to save it".

That is not The Law of Attraction in action. It is, rather, The Law of Doubt. The Law of Attraction can work for you when you have absolute belief that you can achieve your goal. Most of the time you will have no idea exactly how it will come about but, you have full faith and belief that it will happen.

Let's imagine that you have absolute belief in yourself that you can accumulate $30,000 in the time period you have set to accomplish this goal. Having your goal in writing and reviewing it every day, then your mind goes to work to help you achieve it.

You definitely can if you think you can

You begin to notice things that you had never thought of before. Ways for you to make money. You see an opportunity to buy something at a low wholesale price and sell it for a higher price putting the profit aside which moves you closer to your goal. Next, you realize that you have a few things in the garage or attic that you really could do without. You sell these and put the money aside helping you to get closer to your goal. Then, unexpectedly, you get a phone call from someone who was referred to you to do extra work for them on the side. It's part time and won't interfere with your full time work. As each day passes and you move toward the end of the period of time you've set for yourself, opportunities will come to you that will help you achieve your goal. These opportunities present themselves to you because your mind is open and attracts like thoughts.

The Law of Attraction is an amazing gift because it is present with you and goes to work for you when you obey its principles starting with absolute belief. It will present doors of opportunity to you and if you believe that you can achieve your dreams, you will recognize these opportunities and without hesitation, enthusiastically walk through them. However, you are likely to have resistance from your circle of influence that may undermine or worse, sabotage your goals completely. As such, this is a challenge that must be overcome.

The Circle and Its Influence

The fact that opposites attract creates a challenge when one person is predominantly optimistic and the other is pessimistic. The pessimist usually likes to be referred to as a Realist. The Realists, however, do have their place in society. If not, we would all be Evil Knievel attempting to jump the Snake River Canyon.

The successful achievement of your goals will be limited by the collective belief of you and your support group and how you manage that belief.

Those who you rely upon for feedback and support will weigh in on your proposed dreams and goals. Some will be positive and others will offer only negativity. Over the years, previous set-backs and successes will factor into their belief system ultimately affecting how they react to your ideas. Therefore, it is not only your belief system that you must contend with it is the collective belief system of your support group that will be one of your most difficult challenges to overcome.

For example, a close relative advises you not to risk becoming disappointed by trying something you want to do. Their belief system was created by their past experiences and those of others they've observed over the years. Perhaps, their father was a businessman or a Salesman and he constantly tried new things and was largely unsuccessful. This likely caused stress on the family's finances. With your new proposal, they now have a flashback of the same experience repeating itself only this time, they are not a child, they are an observing adult. Their past experiences and observations have created their very own belief system, whether it is either optimistic or mostly pessimistic.

Based on their belief system, if they are negative to your idea, they see all bad experiences as being permanent even if the circumstances are entirely different.

Why do optimistic people see set-backs as momentary and pessimistic people see them as permanent?

Unfortunately, the pessimistic person lacks belief that they can recover from the set-back or that circumstances will change for the better. The pessimistic person cannot see past the set-back and the loss of energy and negative emotions make it seem impossible for them to argue against reality (the reality of the set-back and the circumstances that go with it).

Sadly, it is a matter of being stuck in the past that makes it seem impossible for the pessimistic person to look into the future with any hope. On the other hand, the optimistic person continues to focus on 'what can be' rather than 'what is'. The optimistic person continually visualizes, in their mind, how things can be by putting effort toward their goal.

In many cases, it is not a matter of *your* belief in your dreams that presents the challenge. Often, it is someone in your circle of influence that either helps or hurts your chances for success. Perhaps they are telling you, "It's too risky", "commission Sales is for gamblers", or "What if you don't make any money?" Usually you can identify this type of person because they use the words, 'always' and 'never' on a consistent basis. "We'll *never* get ahead" or "Things *always* seem to go wrong".

Whatever your dream or your goal, you must learn how to help yourself or someone else deal with set-backs. Why? Your circle. Within your circle of family or friends will be someone who is very influential that is the opposite of you. For example, it may be your best friend, your boyfriend, girlfriend, husband, wife, parent, brother, sister or cousin that either encourages or discourages you to move forward with your dreams. No matter the nature of your goal or dream, it is you who must weigh the advantages and disadvantages. When you have someone in your circle of friends or family who may be discouraging you, here is an exercise that can help.

First, sit down with that person and take a sheet of paper or a legal pad and draw a vertical straight line down the middle of the page. Next, on the top left write 'Against' and on the top right add the word, 'For'. Now, at the very top define your goal in one sentence if you can. This will help to keep your goal clearly in focus. Next, ask the person joining you to help come up with reasons why you should not move forward. Write down as many reasons why you should not move forward as you can.

Next, write down as many reasons on the right why you should move forward toward your goal. Do not stop until you have exhausted each and every reason as to why you should move forward.

Finally, after completing this exercise with the other person and if it does, in fact, appear that the 'For' side outweighs the 'Against' side, there is one more exercise you will want to do in order to get the other person on your side and encouraging you to move forward toward your goal. For yourself and the person you are doing this exercise with, you will want to present the consequences of *not moving forward*. If the other person is a pessimist, they have already presented the consequences, as they see it, of moving forward.

Taking the same sheet you used to record the reasons for and against moving forward, under the heading 'For' write down the consequences of not moving forward. Introducing fear of loss will help put it all into perspective. Clearly defining what you will not receive will help the other person to actually weigh the consequences of not moving forward with what they perceive to be the reasons for doing so. Being able to see for themselves with their very own eyes what the options are and the respective consequences can dramatically help your well intentioned support person or group to finally get behind you.

The Law of Attraction is the driving force that pulls the chain of success.

However, if what we have now come to know as 'belief' is not complete, then this necessary link will become weak and will cause all the other links to come apart resulting in your goals and dreams dying out.

The Law of Attraction, therefore, requires absolute belief.

Visualize what it is that you want

Four
Visualization

Visualization is creating a mental picture of your goal, dream or desire. It is as much a part of The Law of Attraction as popcorn is to a movie.

"Visualization is daydreaming with a purpose" – Bo Bennett

"Make sure you visualize what you really want, not what someone else wants for you" – Jerry Gillies

"To accomplish great things we must first dream, then visualize, then plan... believe... act!" – Alfred A. Montapert

"Visualize this thing that you want, see it, feel it, believe in it. Make your mental blue print, and begin to build". – Robert Collier

Visualization is the practice of seeking to affect the outer world by changing our thoughts. The term 'Creative Visualization' is the basic technique underlying positive thinking and is frequently used by athletes to enhance their performance. The concept originally began in the United States with the nineteenth century New Thought movement. One of the first to practice the technique of creative visualization was Wallace Wattles (1860–1911), who wrote *The Science of Getting Rich*.

Creative visualization is the technique of using one's imagination to visualize specific behaviors or events occurring in one's life. Advocates suggest creating a detailed plan of what one desires and then visualizing it over and over again with all of the senses, i.e., Do you see it? Do you feel it? Can you hear it? What does it smell like? For example, in sports a golfer may visualize the "perfect" stroke over and over again to mentally train muscle memory. Visualization helps us to create in our mind exactly what we wish for and desire. Practicing this technique brings our goals to a reality.

Every person who has ever created anything first visualized in their mind precisely what it was that they wanted. Painters, Builders, Architects, even Coaches first visualize what they want to create and, then they go about creating it.

It is true. Everything does start with a dream. Without a dream, nothing of any significance happens. However there is a big difference between dreaming and visualizing. A person must visualize themselves succeeding. One must first see the light at the end of the tunnel through visualization.

Visualizing your goals into thoughts helps you to see their achievement. Visualize the feeling you will experience when you have realized your goal.

To use Visualization, first make a picture of what you want to accomplish in your mind and meditate upon it. Your subconscious mind creates pictures of what you are focusing on. Form the picture in your mind and follow it with strong belief and your mind will work day and night to make your goals and dreams a reality. The power of your mind can literally bring them into existence.

Most people find it difficult to set aside the distractions of living and actually visualize what they really want.

But, if you take time each day to visualize what you really want, then what you are creating in your mind's eye can become a reality. It only takes a few minutes each day to accomplish this necessary task.

If you create it in your mind and constantly focus upon what you have set as a goal for yourself, The Law of Attraction can help bring those thoughts to a reality.

*Achievement of any goal takes place only
after you have decided not to give up*

Five
The Role of Persistence

Talent alone will not create wealth. Knowledge by itself cannot bring about success.

Many Salespeople never achieve success because they throw in the towel too soon. This is particularly sad as their goals could have been reached with one key to success.

It is called, Persistence.

Over the centuries there have been countless men and women who achieved their clear objectives while dealing with obstacles too numerous or challenging to comprehend.

There is someone, however, worth observing who lived during an exciting time in American History.

The period from the late 1800's until the early 1900's.

It was an era known as the Industrial Age and was a time of exponential growth and new opportunity. The man was a physician who lived in Vermont and was married to one of the daughters of the richest men in the state, the founder of *Payne's Celery Compound*, a popular cure-all.

His name was *Horatio Nelson Jackson*. He is the epitome of setting a goal and against all odds choosing to press on until it was eventually achieved. Examining his success demonstrates how you can get what you want by having a clear goal in mind and relentlessly pressing on until you have acquired it.

Horatio was born in 1872 and by the age of thirty-one had become an auto enthusiast. He did not agree with the attitude of the majority who mistakenly assumed that the automobile was a passing fad and only a play toy of the rich. Horatio realized that the automobile was not only here to stay, he saw it becoming an important part of American society.

"I had," he later recalled, "succumbed completely to a primary enthusiasm for the newfangled horseless buggy."

In 1903, while visiting San Francisco's University Club, Horatio wagered $50 that an automobile could cross the country. To many, this would sound like a ridiculous idea as Horatio owned no automobile at the time, had no prior experience driving automobiles much less traversing the country. His wager could also be viewed as foolish given the fact that there were no road maps and, moreover, the entire country at that time consisted of no more than 150 miles of paved roadway.

After sending his wife home to Vermont by train, Horatio met a man by the name of Sewell Crocker. He convinced the experienced bicycle-turned-auto mechanic to accompany him on the long journey.

Crocker accepted the challenge and encouraged Horatio to purchase an automobile manufactured by the Winton Motor Carriage Company. In addition to the Winton, Horatio bought sleeping bags, blankets, cooking utensils, a rifle and shotgun, pistols, canteens and other necessities required for the long trip.

Horatio also took into account the failed cross country attempt by the founder of the Winton Carriage Company, Alexander Winton and decided to take a northerly route through the Sacramento Valley and Oregon Trail instead of the southern approach that required crossing the desert southwest.

In those days, most people traveled no more than twelve miles from their homes. Jackson described the mostly unmarked paths he was forced to bounce over as "a compound of ruts." Leaving San Francisco and after only fifteen miles, their troubles started with a flat tire and, from then on, he and Crocker were alternately working on the car, pulling it out of mud holes, teetering on the edge of cliffs or simply getting lost.

After one harrowing drive over a stretch of narrow, bumpy road in the Cascade Range, the noise of the car covered the fact that the duo's cooking gear had fallen off. Realizing the significance of their loss, Jackson and Crocker determined that "living off the countryside or starving was less to be feared than a return trip," wrote Jackson's friend Ralph Hill in his book, 'The Mad Doctor's Drive.'

Early on in the journey, they were given wrong directions of more than a hundred miles out of their way by a woman who wanted her relatives to see a horseless carriage for the very first time. The excursion was difficult as the Winton broke down constantly and had to be pulled across deep streams by block and tackle. As there were no auto repair shops or hardware stores in existence at the time, Horatio and his companion were stuck in small towns for days at a time waiting for supplies to reach them by train.

After nearly two months of their extraordinary trip, Horatio and his mechanic finally reached New York on July 26, 1903 making history as the first to cross the country in an automobile. His persistence paid off.

Horatio Nelson Jackson is admired for his tenacity and relentless drive to be the first person to cross America in an automobile. His goal was very clear and specific, San Francisco to New York. More importantly, he achieved it through sheer determination and tireless persistence.

One Step At A Time

One of the primary reasons why Salespeople give up too soon is the fact that the task at hand seems overwhelming. How could I ever accomplish this? They ask themselves.

Here is what successful people do; no matter the goal or objective, you can accomplish what you set out to do by taking it one step at a time.

"Take the first step in faith. You don't have to see the whole staircase, just take the first step" – Martin Luther King Jr.

Once your ultimate goal has been clearly defined, focus your attention to your daily, weekly and monthly objectives. If you take one step at a time, the incremental steps that you set for yourself will lead you to where you want to go.

Experiment

Persistence without experimentation can cause you to give up before your goal is reached.

The definition of insanity is, 'something foolish or unreasonable'. To keep doing the same thing over and over again expecting different results is a sure sign of insanity.

Usually, the path to success is not like an interstate highway with easy-on and easy-off ramps. Your pathway has to be defined as you go along and you must also be willing to experiment.

Being persistent with one method usually will not bring success. But, persistence along with an enthusiasm for experimentation can bring about success.

There Is A Way!

People who have a 'never give up' attitude have one distinct quality. They continue to tell themselves, "There must be a way".

If you tell yourself, "I guess this just isn't going to work out", you might as well hang it up. You are destined to fail once you accept defeat. Your mind is like a magnet. It will attract positive thoughts or negative thoughts. If you give up and tell yourself, "There is no way I'm going to make this happen", your mind goes to work, like a magnet, attracting like thoughts.

*Many never succeed because they
throw in the towel too soon*

With negative energy, you will not be able to come up with an alternative solution that could eventually bring about success. Instead, your negative thoughts help to convince you that your decision to quit is the right choice. "Yea, I knew this was going to be too hard" or, "Trying something new is too risky. I'm glad I quit when I did".

On the other hand, when someone tells themselves, "There must be a way", then positive energy causes the mind to explore or brainstorm new ideas or even a new approach that can lead to success.

The key is to believe that you can accomplish your goals and that there has to be a way to make it happen.

Remaining persistent and determined will enable you to continue moving forward until you have achieved your dream.

Get Started

Many are the excuses for those who never step-up to the challenge of visualizing their future and thereafter working to create it.

You don't have to know everything to get started in your quest for success. To reach your goal, you must have a 'learn as you go' mentality.

Do Not Give Up!

Abraham Lincoln went to war a captain and returned a private. Afterward, he was a failure as a businessman. As a lawyer in Springfield, his practice could not be considered a success. He later turned to politics and was defeated in his first attempt at joining the legislature. He was also defeated in his first attempt to be nominated to Congress. He was defeated in his application to be Commissioner of the General Land Office. He was defeated in the Senatorial election of 1854. He was defeated in his efforts for the Vice-Presidency in 1856, and he was soundly defeated in the election of 1858 to become a Senator. He would later write to a friend, "I am now the most miserable man living. If what I feel were equally distributed to the whole human family, there would not be one cheerful face on the earth". Fortunately, however, Abraham Lincoln's legacy as the 16th President of The United States stands as a testament to never giving up.

Without absolute belief and a willingness and enthusiasm to continue experimenting until the goal of inventing the light bulb was reached, where would the light bulb be today had Thomas Edison given up after only 900 attempts?

Winston Churchill failed the sixth grade. He was defeated in every election for public office until he became the Prime Minister of Great Britain at the age of 62. He had the attitude that one should *never give in.*

Albert Einstein was not able to speak until he was 4 and did not read until he was 7. His parents thought he was far from normal.

One of his teachers described him as being mentally slow, unsociable, and forever adrift in foolish dreams.

After famous singer Fred Astaire's first screen test, the memo from the testing director of MGM in 1933, read, "Can't act. Can't sing. Slightly bald. Can dance a little." As a reminder, he kept that memo over the fire place in his Beverly Hills home. Astaire felt that, "when you're experimenting, you have to try so many things before you choose what you want, that you may go days getting nothing but exhaustion." And, if you show relentless persistence, he said, "The higher up you go, the more mistakes you are allowed. Right at the top, if you make enough of them, it's considered to be your style."

At the conclusion of his first audition, Sidney Poitier was told by the casting director, "Why don't you stop wasting people's time and go out and become a dishwasher or something?" Poitier recalled that it was at that moment he had decided to devote his life to acting.

After Harrison Ford's first performance as a hotel bellhop in the film *Dead Heat*, one of the studio chiefs called him to his office. He told Ford, "Sit down kid. I want to tell you a story. The first time Tony Curtis was ever in a movie he delivered a bag of groceries. We took one look at him and knew he was a movie star." The studio chief dismissed Ford with "You ain't got it kid, you ain't got it ... now get out of here."

Michael Jordan was cut from his high school basketball team. Jordan said, "I've failed over and over again in my life. That is why I succeed."

Jerry Seinfeld walked on-stage for the first time at a comedy club and looked out at the audience and froze. He stumbled through his minute and a half of material and was jeered offstage. He returned the following night and closed his routine to wild applause.

Of course, these were not ordinary men but, what made them extraordinary was their 'never give up attitude'.

Their persistence was more valuable than knowledge, skill or even talent.

They pressed on, learned from their mistakes and were finally successful only after failing many times over.

The Law of Attraction can and will help you to succeed if you choose never to give up too soon before your dream is realized.

*To achieve all your dreams,
the glass must be half full*

Six
The Positive Mind

A positive outlook is to The Law of Attraction as water is to a farmer. Without it, the seeds of opportunity cannot grow.

Any goal ever achieved was due to a positive mindset that spawned an idea that grew into a reality.

The Law of Attraction is like a magnet in that like attracts like. What you consistently focus upon becomes your reality.

Just as a farmer relies on steady rain during the growing season, Salespeople who are able to stay positive are far more likely to achieve their goals.

How do you stay positive when obstacles get in the way of accomplishing your hopes and dreams?

What techniques can help someone in Sales to stay positive? And, what can you do to avoid bouts of negative thinking?

Optimism Creates Success

The word *optimism* literally means 'an inclination to put the most favorable meaning upon actions and events or to anticipate the best possible outcome'.

An optimistic person is generally able to possess a positive outlook because they see events working out in their favor. They also see unfortunate circumstances as temporary in nature and success as being potentially permanent.

Conversely, a pessimistic person sees unfortunate circumstances as permanent and success as temporary. "Well, just enjoy the good times while you can, because they never last."

The pessimist sees no hope while the optimist embraces hope.

No matter how difficult your career in Sales can get or how impossible things seem to be, the optimist recognizes that opportunity is just around the corner.

Why? Because when a Salesperson keeps on working, believes in The Law of Attraction and makes every effort to look for doors of opportunity, things do work out. Circumstances do change for the better if you attract positive events due to a positive frame of mind and a hopeful attitude.

Hope as a Motivator

The word *hope* literally means, "To cherish an idea with anticipation".

There is a lot of meaning in those words. Therefore, let's break them down to better understand how hope can make your dreams a reality.

First, the word *cherish* means, 1: to hold dear, feel or show affection for (*cherished* her friends): to keep or cultivate with care and affection: nurture (*cherishes* his marriage), 2: to entertain or harbor in the mind deeply and resolutely (still *cherishes* that memory).

When we *cherish* our goal, it is constantly on our mind. We *hold it dear* in that we think about it constantly. A goal is *nurtured* when we make daily decisions that move us toward it. We also *harbor* our goal in that we keep it close or tethered so that our goal doesn't drift away and ceases to become our hope.

When we *harbor* our goal deeply into our mind and nurture it, we are then able to consistently build upon it.

Hope becomes an ally for The Law of Attraction in that by constantly thinking upon your goal, cherishing it and nurturing your desire, the goal eventually becomes a reality in your mind before you have even acquired it.

How To Stay Positive

A few years ago, I set a goal that I eagerly wanted to achieve. Therefore, one of the first things I did was to find a map that would help me achieve my goal. The map, which represented the area into which I would accomplish my goal, was hung on a particular wall where I could easily see it.

Every day, I couldn't help but look at the map which had colored pins that marked my progress. As the number of pins grew, the more my goal became a reality. Looking at the map every day helped me to stay positive. Even though obstacles arrived, the map just stared at me, daring me to succeed!

Each and every day, the portions of the map that were not occupied with pins seemed to cry out, 'what are you waiting on', and that helped to keep me positive as well as motivated to achieve what was the absolute desire of reaching my goal. There are many ways to stay positive and most of all, motivated. Here are a few more suggestions.

1. Whatever your goal is, the house you want or the car you want to drive, take a picture of it and place it where you see it every day. *Think Screen Saver!*

2. If your goal is money. Write yourself a check for the specific amount you want and include the date you want to cash it. Put it in a place you will see it each and every day. This will keep you completely focused and will drive you to achieve your goal.

3. Write your goal on a business card and carry it in your pocket or purse where you will stumble across it during the day. You will be surprised how motivated you will become.

4. Write your goals down on a sheet of paper and vow to look at it daily, weekly, monthly and yearly.

5. Take time each day to reflect upon your goal. Imagine already achieving it. How will your life change? What will it be like if you do not achieve your goal?

Attitude: Ally or Enemy?

In case you haven't heard this expression today, I'll refresh your memory. Here it is, *Your attitude determines your altitude.*

It's one of the most widely used expressions that reveals the role that attitude plays in order to create success.

But, what does it really mean? Do we understand it fully?

Sometimes a phrase can be used so often that the meaning or import is watered down or completely lost. It certainly appears to be the case with this expression.

So, let's break it down and understand the real meaning behind this commonly used phrase.

The word *Attitude* means; 1) a mental position with regard to a fact or state and, 2) a feeling or emotion toward a fact or state. Therefore, your attitude is a mental state but, has its roots in one's emotions.

Your attitude really is a matter of how you feel about something. 1) If you feel that you never received the education you think you deserved then your attitude is affected. 2) If you feel that your boss is not fair in dealing with you, your attitude is affected. 3) If you feel that others seem to always have the advantage, for whatever reason, again your attitude is affected.

This phenomenon, how your attitude is affected by your feelings which turn into thoughts, is called *Spillover*.

Spillover occurs when positive or negative emotions spill over into another time, event or place. For example, imagine you lost a very large customer account, you then had a flat tire on the way home, and your cell phone was turned off by the phone company for non-payment. After experiencing these three negative events back-to-back, you arrive home only to kick the dog off the porch for nothing more than simply getting in your way.

Spillover.

The way in which you manage your emotions will determine whether you allow one set of negative emotions from one particular bad event to spill over into another.

How can this be done? How can you manage your emotions effectively? The key to managing your emotions and, therefore, eliminating *Spillover* is to refuse to allow negative thoughts to *move in*. Refusing negative thoughts and replacing them with opposing arguments can help you to stay positive.

Refuse Negative Thoughts

Your mind works like a powerful search engine as it goes crawling about validating and supporting your beliefs or convictions.

If you allow negative thoughts to enter your mind, the powerful search engine goes to work looking for facts, examples, case history or circumstances that prove what the negative mind has already chosen to believe. For example, if you tell yourself that you have no chance to be the top Salesperson in your company, then your thoughts become a self-fulfilled prophecy. Your mind will attract similar thoughts that support the predisposed belief. So, how do you fight negative thinking either from your own doubts or the doubts expressed by others?

You reject them! Let your mind do the heavy lifting. Allow your mind to look for facts that disprove any negative thinking.

Every single time a negative thought enters your mind, it's as if you come to a "Y" in the road and you must decide which direction to take. Of course, the easy choice is to veer right since you're on the right side of the road anyway, just the same as it is easy to stay on the negative side of your mind when it has introduced a negative thought. But, you do have a choice and it's simply a matter of choosing one over the other, positive versus negative.

Take the time to meditate and allow your mind to come up with reasons why you can be the top Salesperson.

What if you could listen in to someone's inner thoughts as they argue against negative thinking? You would hear something like this:

"Wow, an extra one thousand dollars for being the top Salesperson this month! You know, I could really use the extra cash. I need to put more in savings and redecorating the living room is something we've been planning for months. It's just, well, I don't know if I can do it. Wow, I'd have to increase my Sales by almost 50%. Geez! How could I ever do that? I don't have all the contacts everyone else has. I've only been in town six months. Some of the Salespeople have lived here all their life. It's not even a contest when I don't have the advantages everyone else has.

Do you see how the mind can easily choose negativity

when one has approached the 'Y' in the road when explaining to themselves why they can or cannot achieve a specific goal?

Everyone experiences negative thoughts. No one is exempt. The solution to addressing negative thinking is a matter of what you actually do once those negative thoughts have entered your conscious mind.

Negative thoughts are like garbage. Nasty, smelly, rotten garbage. They're unhealthy and will hinder your ultimate success. Negative thoughts can and will make you mentally sick.

What can you do to keep negative thoughts from creating more negativity in your life and in your career?

You have to take action.

You have to get off the couch and take the garbage out. You have to reject each and every negative thought. Listen in as the person we've been listening to argues against negative thinking.

"Wait a minute! So what if everyone else knows more people, I'm the one that's more likable. I know I have just as much talent as anyone else and I'm making the same number of cold calls as everyone else but, I know I can network and get more referrals. Ok, let's figure this out. I need to close 50% more Sales this month. So, last month I closed 40 Sales which obviously means, that I need 20 more for a total of 60 to win the $1000 dollars. Now, let's see, what is my closing ratio? Well, it's been running about 1 out of 3. That means I need to talk to 180

customers instead of 120 or I need to close more. I think I can do both which means that I've got to stop taking those long lunches and I need to use my cell phone more between calls. I think that can work!"

You have that ability to argue against negative thinking the same as the person in the above example. It's really a matter of whether you choose to or not. It's up to you. Refuse negative thoughts and allow your mind to explore the possibilities as to what you can accomplish.

Don't Forget Your Tools

Imagine for a moment that you build houses for a living. Obviously, you have the tools of the trade, hammer, saw, power drill, and various other necessary tools to help you get the job done.

What are some of the more important tools in Sales?

Your goal is like a hammer. How could a builder be expected to craft something out of wood if there were no hammer? It would be very difficult.

Without a clearly defined goal in which to strive for, it is very difficult to stay positive and focused. You're asking too much from yourself if you have no goal in mind.

Your thoughts are like a powerful saw. Not the hand held type, I'm talking about the electric circular saw. When sharp, this saw can rip through just about anything. When your mind is positive and sharp, you can accomplish anything you set out to do. If, you allow your

Your mind attracts thoughts that support your belief

mind to become dull from negative thinking, your mind will not have the energy to even try. It will be too dull to cut through the challenges you will face as you attempt to move on toward your goal.

So, how do you keep your mind positive and sharp?

1) By keeping your goals clearly in mind and reviewing them every day. Reject negative thinking and replace them with positive thoughts.

2) You can do this by arguing to yourself why you can accomplish your goals.

Always keep your tools close at hand and keep them sharp and in good working order. If you do, you will allow The Law of Attraction to help you receive what you desire most, the absolute realization and achievement of your goals and dreams.

Feed Your Mind A Positive Diet

A positive mental outlook is the cornerstone of The Law of Attraction. A positive attitude opens your mind when The Law of Attraction presents doors of opportunity. Your positive mind not only allows you the opportunity to actually see the door, it will give you the energy and drive to *seize the day* as it were and to walk through it.

About half of your tendency to think positively is genetic and the other half comes from life experiences and how you reacted to those experiences. However, today is the first day of the rest of your life when considering the power of The Law of Attraction.

Successful Salespeople regularly feed their mind positive food. What you put in will without fail generate what comes out. If you feed your mind positive thoughts regularly, then it will be easier for you to stay positive and focused on your target.

Attend Audio University

If you commute daily or if you drive a vehicle calling on accounts, you have a tremendous opportunity to feed your mind a positive diet of useful information that will help you to become successful in Sales.

It is called *Audio University*.

Every day in which you commute to work or drive around making Sales calls is an excellent opportunity to attend *Audio University*. The most effective way anyone can accomplish something is through *incremental progression*. Obviously, you cannot eat a whole pie in a single bite. However, you can accomplish the task one piece at a time.

Success is achieved by the amount of knowledge you acquire and what you ultimately do with that knowledge. Over time, you can increase your knowledge bank by incrementally listening to audio programs.

Audio University is a place in which to expand your level of education that you create on your own right inside your car, van, truck or suv or through public transportation. Take the time each day to listen to audio programs that help to feed your mind a positive diet. Most of the very best self-help books and Sales training programs are available on audio. Just thirty minutes or more a day over a period of time can dramatically improve your rate of success.

Incremental progression can work for you if you take the time each and every day to attend *Audio University*.

What should you listen to?

Your weakest link in the chain of success will limit the amount of success you achieve. Therefore, determine what you need first that will enable you to strengthen your weakest link.

For example, let's imagine that your weakest link is the inability to take action. You constantly procrastinate. Obviously, you need an audio program that will help you to eliminate procrastination. Therefore, visit your local bookstore or go online and search for an audio program that will feed you mental food that will help you to avoid procrastination. The title, Procrastination Elimination by Susan Lynn Perry is available in Audio book format (audio CD) at, www.InterSkillMedia.com. Choose the Products icon and make your selection.

Take the time to examine yourself to determine what your strengths and weaknesses are.

Give yourself the gift of a steady diet of mental food that will help you to keep your mind positive. Attend *Audio University* every day knowing that you will never graduate the school of higher learning. The Law of Attraction can guide you to countless doors of opportunity. However, you will want to make the most of these opportunities by strengthening all aspects of your personality, selling techniques and strategies.

Action is Control in Disguise

To keep yourself in a constant positive mental state, we've seen how optimism, hope, refusing negative thoughts, setting clearly define goals together with a steady diet of positive mental food can help you to create the best opportunity for success in Sales.

However, there is one more item that should be included that can make all the above much easier to achieve. It was discussed in an earlier chapter but, it is an absolute difference maker. It's like a battery charger that breathes energy into everything you do. It's called *control*.

Your mental state, level of anxiety and life satisfaction is directly linked to the degree of *control* you have at any given time.

How can its effect or its power be described? Let's expand on an earlier example.

Imagine you're on vacation with family that includes a teenage relative who just received their driving permit three days before the scheduled trip to the mountains of Colorado. Now, imagine it's your second day there and you and your relatives are driving over a mountain pass to go fishing and later on for a bit of hiking. Because there were other adults present and the vehicle is not your own, you had decided to ride in the back seat directly behind the driver. It was not a big deal as you would still be able to see the country side from such a strategic vantage point.

At the last minute, however, the teenager earlier mentioned got the bright idea of wanting to drive and somehow, is now behind the wheel driving down the steep road faster than you are comfortable with. As you see the speedometer climb, your heart beats even faster. Your palms begin to sweat and you're now on the edge of your seat hoping that the teenager's driving course was conducted by a qualified instructor and, hopefully, the three days of driving experience was helpful.

At this point, is your anxiety level at an all time high due to a lack of food? No. Not enough sleep? No. Fading eyesight? No.

It is a simple matter of a complete lack of *control*. Do you think that any reasonable passenger in this situation could think clearly? Manage his or her emotions? Set clearly defined goals and work toward them or even create a positive environment? Of, course not. When you are in a situation where you feel that you have a complete loss of control, the wheels begin to fall off.

The degree of control you have at any given moment determines your level of anxiety and satisfaction.

When you have a sense of *control*, you're able to manage your emotions, think more positively, set goals and work toward them. You are also able to create a positive environment in which success can be achieved.

How then, can you establish a significant degree of control in your life as well as your Sales career? *Action*. When you are moving forward you feel a sense of control. It is as if you are now behind the wheel rather than someone else less qualified. Planning your work and then working your plan gives you a sense of control necessary to creating a positive environment as well as a positive state of mind.

When you stop making follow-up calls, stop cold calling, stop measuring yourself, stop networking, and stop smiling at customers, all of these create a negative effect that will then give you a feeling of a loss of control. *Action* reduces fear and boosts a confident outlook that is positive. When you are moving forward, good things happen. Like attracts like and your reality becomes what your dominant thoughts are. When you stop and allow anxiety and negative thinking to take over, The Law of Attraction will attract more of what you do not want. Because of your anxiety, negative thoughts will inevitably attract more anxiety.

Make sure to create for yourself a daily, weekly and monthly plan of action. It can be as simple as writing down a list each day of what you want to accomplish for that day and scoring each item on the list in order of priority and importance.

If, at the end of the day, you have any remaining tasks that were not completed, then make sure that you include any unfinished tasks on your list for the next day.

This will help you to feel much more confident and positive about yourself and your goals and dreams. Moving forward and taking action, along with a positive mind, will help you to create your own future.

*The state of being grateful is a key
factor in The Law of Attraction*

Seven
Gratitude

I recall my six grade teacher, Mrs. Rains. Everyone has a favorite teacher. She was the epitome of kindness and fairness.

Mrs. Rains would start the day by standing in front of the wide chalkboard and wipe away any trace of the day before. If you didn't copy the homework, you had better ask another student. No one was brave enough to ask her. It wasn't that she was mean. It was the opposite. She was very kind and you simply didn't want to disappoint her.

Looking back and seeing her wipe away all traces of the day before on that chalkboard reminds me of a key element in the Law of Attraction.

The element or principle is that of *Gratitude*.

When Mrs. Rains wiped away the homework and studies from the day before and focused on today's work, she unknowingly provided a lesson in learning and applying the principles of the Law of Attraction.

You see, The Law of Attraction is a matter of focusing upon today and letting go of the past.

Gratitude and the exercise of reflecting on what we have rather than what we do not have is a key component in experiencing the power of the Law of Attraction.

When you wipe away the past by being grateful and, therefore, reflect upon what you do have instead of what you do not have, enables you to think positively about the future and attracts positive energy to you. Letting the past and any associated negativity to dominate your thoughts obstructs the positive energy that is necessary to attract what you do want rather than what you do not want.

Gratitude is like a thermostat. It helps you control your mind-set and helps you to maintain a positive frame of mind. This positive mental environment allows thoughts and ideas to grow and is the positive force that attracts like thoughts.

Negative thoughts about the past, limits the subconscious belief necessary to accomplish your goal or dream. Negative thoughts will also obstruct your vision. Like bugs on a windshield obstructing your view, negative thoughts keep you from focusing upon what you want to accomplish and achieve.

Gratitude, on the other hand, enables you to remove any negative thoughts and helps you to keep them from robbing you of the energy and enthusiasm necessary to attract more positive thoughts.

"Many people who order their lives rightly in all other ways are kept in poverty by their lack of gratitude" – Wallace Wattles

In Sales, it is very easy to focus upon what you do not have.

"Oh, man! It never fails. Just when I think I'm getting ahead, I lose another account and now, I'm going to lose more commissions".

This example illustrates what happens when Gratitude is left out of The Law of Attraction equation.

This does not mean that we should not measure our success or that goals should not be used to inspire us. On the contrary, it is through measurement that we can achieve extraordinary results in our life and in our career. It is Gratitude, however, that keeps our frame of mind in check and creates the necessary mental environment that breeds and attracts more positive thoughts and, ideas that spur us onto success.

Lack of Gratitude breeds and attracts negative emotions and is the cornerstone of a pessimistic attitude which in turn attracts more of the same.

It is primarily those who are ungrateful that are unhappy. These individuals are walking negative wildfires burning every positive thought or emotion in their path. It is imperative that you avoid these people at all costs for they will turn your positive thoughts and dreams into ashes.

Avoiding these people is easier said than done. We may work or even live with these negative thinkers.

If you are a positive person trying to apply The Law of Attraction in your life and in your career and you do work or live around these wildfires, either change the subject or walk away until their fire has been extinguished or cannot jump the road and burn down your positive and grateful mind-set.

The dictionary defines Gratitude as the state of being thankful. This word means that one is "conscious of the benefit received".

Gratefulness or Gratitude has, therefore, the connotation of being aware of the benefits received from what we have or possess. In no dictionary will you find where gratitude or thankfulness is linked to what we do not have. They are like water and oil and do not mix. They have no relationship with each other, whatsoever.

That is why a person who is seeking The Law of Attraction must work at maintaining a positive mental attitude while expressing thankfulness and Gratitude.

Express Gratitude Daily

"The daily practice of gratitude is one of the conduits by which your wealth will come to you" – Wallace Wattles

Some have the habit of getting up in the morning and reflecting upon, with Gratitude, the opportunity of a new day. Others reflect upon what they are grateful for at other times.

In any case, make the process of being grateful a daily routine. Never let anything or anyone stop you from showing Gratitude. By demonstrating a thankful and grateful attitude, you become like the farmer who constantly tills the ground, making it fertile for continuous growth. This is the key to The Law of Attraction.

*In order to influence others, one must be
perceived as having already achieved success*

Eight
The Cues of Influence

Customers are influenced by Salespeople who are perceived to be competent, capable and intelligent. If not, the Salesperson's words will carry very little weight.

The challenge every Salesperson faces is to get the customer to not only believe his or her words, but also to be influenced by them. Generally speaking, people do not automatically take the words of a Salesperson at face value. A Salesperson's words are filtered or discounted.

Why? First and foremost, you are a Salesperson and the customer knows you are paid a commission to sell and, therefore, are biased.

Imagine that you wanted to learn how to hit a golf ball and you could ask anyone in the world to teach you how and money was not an object. Who would you ask? Go ahead and write the person's name below and rate them.

_____   _____

Name   Rating

If you were to measure their words, on a scale of 1 to 10 with 10 being the most believable, how would you rate the person you chose? Did you rate them a 10? If you did, it was your absolute belief that their words would certainly influence how you would hit your next golf ball. As a Salesperson, customers subconsciously rate your words on a scale of 1 to 10 with 10 being the highest.

Based upon your past experience, go ahead and write your name and rate yourself on a scale of 1 to 10.

_____   _____
Your Name   Rating

The secret to influencing a customer's behavior is a matter of knowing how to make your words more believable.

Unfortunately, the majority of books that teach the art of selling focus primarily upon word tracks and Sales strategies, but leave out the most critical element in Sales, *The Cues of Influence.*

While word tracks and Sales strategies are a necessary component to successful selling, nonetheless, if a customer does not perceive the Salesperson to be competent, capable or intelligent, no set of words or Sales strategy will help close the sale. For example, if a Salesperson's shirt is wrinkled or even soiled and the result is a shoddy appearance, will the customer perceive the Salesperson to be competent, capable or more importantly, intelligent? It is very unlikely.

The customer may buy from a Salesperson with a wrinkled or soiled shirt but, if the price is negotiable, then the customer will likely want a lower price or will take the opportunity to look elsewhere. This is a key element that every Salesperson cannot overlook.

If, on the other hand, the Salesperson that is professionally dressed communicates, validates and artfully justifies the value of the product or service then, the customer is more likely to be open to doing business. Customers will not respect or value the Salesperson any more than the Salesperson respects or values his or her self. Therefore, the way a Salesperson is dressed will significantly impact what a customer is willing to pay for a product or service.

Dress for Success

In order to influence others, one must be perceived as having already achieved success. The way you dress, the quality of clothing you choose, whether your shoes are shined or not, all factor into a perception that either reinforces your words or detracts.

With most companies, the commissioned Salesperson who dresses the best generally earns the most.

The key factor for a Salesperson is the ability to influence a customer's decision to purchase the product or service offered. Therefore, the Salesperson that is impeccably dressed has a distinct advantage.

The customer is more likely to listen and to be influenced.

In today's selling environment, customers generally discount a Salesperson's words or will certainly be taken with a grain of salt if the Salesperson's words sound like a pitch.

The customer knows that a Salesperson is paid on commission and stereotypically will say anything to get the sale. Therefore, everything you say is already in the works to be discounted. "Of course he's going to say that, he makes a commission if we decide to buy".

Knowing this is all the more reason to exceed the customer's expectations by being the best dressed Salesperson in your company or firm and by providing excellent customer service. Customers want to do business with Salespeople who appear to be successful. So, by all means, take the time to check your dress and grooming.

The Optimum Dress for Men

There is no reality, only perception and the color of your clothing can make a significant impact upon how your customer treats and respects you.

What are the best colors to wear when selling your product or service? First, a lot will depend upon the industry you work in. No matter the item of clothing, your shirt, your pants, your belt, even the way you wear your hair, all of them make a statement. Without even a word spoken, the professional makes a statement that says; I am competent, I am capable, I am smart, I am the Salesperson that any customer can respect and would want to do business with. Conversely, the statement could say, I am not confident, I am not capable, I am not competent. As this topic is critical to your success, take time to study what the most successful people in your industry are wearing and copy their dress and grooming.

In many areas of the country, the fad is to dress down. Some Salespeople in those areas are wearing a polo shirt and khaki slacks or even shorts. That may be true in your area but, a word of caution; just because it may be the fad, ask yourself, what is the age group of my customer base and what are their expectations.

You can never go wrong by asking.

Now, let's get back to colors. The best color that has the greatest impact upon a Salesperson's ability to influence a customer is white. Why? When a male Salesperson wears a pressed white shirt and a tie, it creates the appearance that he is more capable and qualified. This can be especially important if you are new and not a seasoned Salesperson in your industry. A white shirt, in the customer's mind, makes you look like a Manager with a higher degree of authority.

In the customer's mind, a Manager is more likely to treat them with respect, not waste their precious time, have ready answers to their questions and more importantly, the customer feels recognized and special when dealing with a Manager.

Not long ago, I met a Salesman who was also working part-time delivering pizza. I admire him for his tenacity and drive to succeed in supporting his family, no matter what he had to do. He soon discovered how to receive customer tips that were double, triple and even quadruple the average tip. He recalled the second day on the job. He was running late and didn't have time to change into more casual and comfortable clothes which was the norm for most pizza delivery drivers. He said that upon his first delivery that particular day, the customer was surprised that a Manager had made a special trip and subsequently gave him a generous tip. At first, he wasn't sure what the customer meant until he got back into his delivery car and realized it was the white shirt and tie!

The lesson here is very clear. Customers perceive your level of self-esteem, self-worth, self-confidence, your level of competence and not to mention, your level of rank, by the manner in which you dress.

The part-time pizza delivery and full-time Salesperson did not dress in a shabby looking white shirt. When he relayed the above story, he was wearing a pressed white shirt and tie. The same outfit he now wears everyday to deliver pizza. Instead of saying to himself, Woe is me! I'm the unlucky guy who has to deliver pizza, he took that lesson to heart and, based upon his new insight, he will take that lesson and earn significant income in the future.

The Law of Attraction creates doors of opportunity.

However, these doors are not marked as success doors. Some of the doors are lesson doors and the more you walk through these doors, the closer you will get to the much sought after success doors. Recently, I conducted a simple experiment to determine the effect that a white shirt and tie would have with customers as compared to other colored shirts with no tie. I had a young man in his early-twenties who wanted to begin a career in Sales. At the time, I knew a Sales Manager at a retail store who needed Salespeople. He preferred experience but, he said, "if you find someone worth giving a chance who is willing to learn, send them over". So I did. But first, I had the young man cut his hair to a professional length and dress in a nicely pressed white

*Customers will value you only to the level
that you value yourself*

shirt and tie, dress pants and shoes. I learned that the Sales Manager was in a meeting until a certain time so I sent the prospective Salesperson over thirty minutes early which would cause him to have to wait in the lobby. Waiting there during that half-hour, the young man was approached by five new customers thinking he was an employee of the retail store even though there were five other Salespeople nearby wearing polo shirts with bright and shiny logos above the pocket. Sure enough, as I had hoped to prove from my experiment, the customers thought that the young man was a Manager and approached him asking questions. Professionally dressed, the young man appeared to be more competent and more capable than the other five employees. Wearing the white shirt and tie, he also had the appearance of someone having authority. After he was hired, I shared with him my experiment and he now wears a white shirt most of the time and especially each Saturday, the store's busiest day.

This does not mean that you need to run out and purchase a whole new wardrobe. Wearing a white shirt and tie every single day can become tiresome and eventually might feel like a uniform. What is important is the fact that you must understand the importance of looking your very best on a consistent basis. Not some of the time but, all the time. So, whether you're wearing white, blue, green or tan, make the most of your success wearing the type of clothing that sends the right message to your customers that will influence their buying decisions.

The Optimum Dress for Women

As a man, I do not pretend to be an expert on women's

clothing, however, after interviewing more than 7,000 people and after training more than 1,500 for a career in Sales, I have met a lot of women who either were not meant to be in Sales or who went on to become successful in Sales. From my experience, there are a number of things that stand out as difference makers for women. The color and type of clothing, how they wear their hair, make-up, jewelry and the way they carry themselves.

First, let's discuss color and type of clothing. Depending upon the industry and the established norms, any woman would be wise to look at the industry associations website and see if there are any pictures of women who play a key role as a leader in that particular industry. This recommendation is only meant to be a starting point. It is possible that the President of the Association is currently on the run and hiding out from the fashion police.

Next, look at the most successful women in your industry and follow their example. However, you may reason, "But, they are already successful and there's just no way I can afford expensive clothes". Good point but, not an excuse. With clothing, it is not the quantity of clothing than matters but, the quality. If you can only afford one or two quality outfits, then start there. Wear your best outfits on the days that matter the most, such as cold calling new customers or making an important business presentation.

Start a fashion fund of your own and set aside the weekly or even daily $5 Vanilla Latte from the local CoffeeBucks. You will be surprised how quickly those little dollars add up as you won't have the worry or guilt of putting your new purchase on a credit card. With peace of mind, you'll buy with a higher sense of self-esteem and self-worth.

What color works best? That depends upon your skin color. Believe me, there are experts out there who can help. Listen to family, friends or business associates who tell you when you look good. Too often, what we think looks good really doesn't, so listen, really listen to those who unselfishly offer comments about your choice of colors and outfit.

Next, is the type of clothing that helps or can even hurt your chance to succeed. Many women are wearing business suits that help to create a perception of confidence, capableness and success. It really is a matter of industry norm whether you wear pants or a dress. Remember, the best dressed Salesperson is likely to earn a higher income than the rest.

In many cases, Salespeople, men and women alike, get too comfortable wearing ordinary or even sloppy clothing and they wonder why they're not earning the kind of money other Salespeople achieve. To earn more, you have to achieve more and, therefore, reach for higher ground.

The type of clothing you wear will definitely have an impact upon your customers. Notice how they are treating you. When they talk to you, do you hear the sound of respect in their voice? If not, there is something about you that is not earning their respect.

From time to time, I meet individuals who want an

opportunity to earn more and, after looking at different career opportunities, they choose to give Sales a chance. In most cases and, other than church, they've rarely dressed up in a shirt and tie. So, I have them go to at least a dozen stores or even the mall to see how people respond to someone who dresses professionally. Interestingly, they all come back surprised by the way they were treated. "What do you mean?" - I usually ask. They proceed to explain that they're not used to being treated with such respect. For some of the men, they had never experienced someone holding the door open for them.

It is a great lesson to see the difference in the way you are treated by your dress and grooming.

As stated beforehand, to be treated with respect, you must respect yourself first. Male or female, you cannot ask someone to treat you better than you treat yourself.

Hair and make-up are both important factors for women in Sales. Wearing your hair long or short is really a matter of personal taste but, you will want to create an impression of professional taste and also one of maturity.

Your make-up is also a matter of personal choice. Nevertheless, having interviewed hundreds of women over the years, I've noticed that some women just do not know how to either apply make-up or actually know the right shade that best suits their skin tone. Fortunately, there are cosmetic consultants such as Avon and Mary Kay who have the expertise in helping anyone achieve the right choice when it comes to make-up. Take advantage of their expertise. Tell them precisely what you are looking for. Tell them the type of customers you come into contact with and let them guide you.

Jewelry is also a way to create a level of success. If your jewelry is in good taste and doesn't distract the sale, then a high level of professionalism can be maintained. How much jewelry is too much? Here are a few tips. First, a ring on each finger is too much. Yes, I've interviewed some women who are walking jewelry stores. It was definitely a distraction. Remember to keep it simple yet, tasteful.

The way you carry yourself also creates a perception of success with customers. How you walk makes a statement about you whether you realize it or not. Always walk with a sense of purpose with your shoulders back and your chin up. Maintaining an erect posture will help you to not only look confident but, you will actually feel more confident.

For more information regarding these and other body language techniques that can dramatically help you to master the art of nonverbal communication, you are invited to visit; www.InterSkillMedia.com. The DVD entitled, *Success and Confidence for Women* is a very informative video that can help you to achieve success in Sales.

Voice Tone Creates Confidence

Research has shown that 38% of all communication is the tone of your voice. The degree to which you are able to influence a customer is due, in large part, by the tone of your voice.

Imagine your favorite movie star for a moment.

If the character they are playing is supposed to be confident and strong, you would expect their voice tone to match. The tone of their voice would convey power and confidence. But, what if the tone of their voice was weak and also lacked necessary confidence, would you believe their character to be real?

Probably not. The same is true in Sales.

You will have a difficult time convincing or, more importantly, *influencing* your customer if the tone of your voice is weak.

In the chapter entitled, *Body Language*, pay attention to the exercise to help you create *The Confident Voice*.

It will enable you to influence your customer's buying decision and move you further down the road toward success in Sales.

Likeable people are more likely to succeed

Nine
The Power of Likeability

Successful Salespeople are likeable. An appealing personality has more influence on opportunity for income than product knowledge.

Salespeople who are likeable can succeed when experience or technical knowledge is lacking.

Likeability starts when a Salesperson likes working with customers and genuinely desires to satisfy their wants and needs.

A likeable Salesperson is able to produce positive emotions in any customer helping them to feel good about the total buying experience and while making them feel good about themselves.

When a customer is faced with two competing Salespeople for the same product or service, the likable Salesperson usually wins their business.

Everyone wants to be around energetic and enthusiastic people and customers are no different. Enthusiastic and likeable people make life easier and the majority of customers take their business to another company when faced with rudeness from an employee.

When a customer likes the messenger, they also tend to believe the message. Therefore, in order to influence customers to make buying decisions, here are a few tips that will help you to be more likable.

First, a successful Salesperson does not take a cynical approach toward customers nor do they believe that 'buyers are liars'. You cannot have a lack of trust for people in general and be likable at the same time. Most every successful Salesperson enjoys interacting and helping customers, therefore, never allow negative thinking to corrupt your view of people. Certainly there are customers that are to be avoided. We help them and then we move on but, taking a dim view of people in general and treating them negatively only hinders The Law of Attraction.

Always believe that people have the best intentions and The Law of Attraction and its doors of opportunity will open to you.

Second, a likeable person also displays the genuine smile. You must be genuine when greeting people. Genuine smiles involve the entire face and will reveal wrinkles around the corner of the eyes. People can tell a fake smile from a genuine smile. If they feel that you are not sincere, the words that you are speaking will carry very little weight. A sincere smile says you are friendly and likeable.

Smiling is a very powerful body language cue and, when greeting someone, will create a reciprocal bounce back affect. This means that giving someone a smile will usually cause them to smile back. Getting your customer to smile makes them feel more at ease and more comfortable with you.

Next, a Salesperson is a personality. Customers must have a sense of motivation to do business with someone. I recently interviewed an individual who wanted to begin a career in Sales with no prior experience. But, this person displayed no personality. There were no lights on in the house. It was as if the person wasn't plugged in and the power cord lay on the ground, some six inches from the electrical outlet. No life. No energy. No enthusiasm.

Nothing.

The Law of Attraction works best when the Salesperson is perceived to be likable, full of life, energy and enthusiasm.

Finally, making a commission in Sales is like making a withdrawal from a bank. However, you must make a deposit beforehand. Your deposit is the way you treat people, and how you deal with them. Likable Salespeople understand that customers are always seeking to justify their purchase with value and when a customer likes the Salesperson and their product or service, then part of the value is the Salesperson and price becomes less of an issue.

The Power of Recognition

Many years ago, the Carnegie Institute of Technology concluded that fifteen percent of a person's success was due to technical knowledge and skill while *eighty-five percent* of success was the result of one's ability to influence people. The secret then to influencing others is *The Power of Recognition*.

Every human has an intrinsic desire to feel needed, wanted and to be recognized. It is a basic human desire we all have for our individuality, our efforts and our success to be acknowledged.

Les Giblin in his book, "How to have Confidence and Power in Dealing with People," masterfully put it this way: "The most universal trait of mankind – a trait you and everybody else have – a trait so strong that it makes men do the things that they do, good and bad – is the desire to be important, the desire to be recognized.." Remember the more important you make people feel, the more they will respond to you."

It is not a matter of flattering someone. *The Power of Recognition* creates a positive environment when recognition is genuine. Effective listening plays a key role in your ability to influence each and every customer. By listening to their specific set of requirements or circumstances, you are giving them the attention they seek. When they see that you understand what they feel are their unique requirements and, you treat them as unique then, the customer will open up and allow you to direct them to make the right choice of product or service. When you make a customer feel important and acknowledge them, you then create an opportunity to influence their buying decisions. When a customer is made to feel important and appreciated, the customer will feel motivated to reward you with the purchase of your product or service.

The Power of Recognition includes acknowledging the customer, complimenting them, using their name and, showing respect by listening for their true wants and needs.

*When a customer likes the messenger,
they also tend to believe the message*

It is not only the fact that a customer wants to feel important, on the other hand, they want to feel that their importance is recognized and acknowledged.

In order for your actions to truly have an impact upon your customer, you must first convince yourself that they really are important. Words alone will not create genuineness and sincerity on your part.

Thinking that they really are important and following through with your actions will create an unbreakable bond between you and your lifetime customer.

I recently went to a major hotel on business. As I walked to the front desk to check in, I noticed the desk clerk was on the phone. Expecting to wait while the clerk answered a customer's question, I was surprised to hear the clerk stop and say, "Yes, I understand. I have a customer waiting, could I call you back in a few minutes? Thank you very much. Bye."

Needless to say I was shocked. I wasn't expecting the desk clerk to even acknowledge me until she had concluded the phone call, which is usually the case.

Here, the desk clerk showed respect to both customers. By acknowledging my presence and letting the other customer know of my presence made me feel important. Then, addressing my requests, she said my name twice and also complimented me on the city in which I was from. She said she had been there on vacation and enjoyed the sites. By her actions, I felt important and appreciated. If she had asked if I would like an upgrade for a few dollars more, who knows, I probably would have taken her up on the suggestion. When *The Power of Recognition* is at work, the price of your product or service becomes secondary.

Yes, everyone wants to be acknowledged, accepted and appreciated. As human beings, we all look for the V.I.P. treatment. Most of the time, it's a matter of affordability. However, treating your customer as important and giving them the recognition that they desire will never cost you anything.

The Magic's in the Name

Everyone loves the sound of their name and when a Salesperson uses the customer's name, something magical happens.

Customers not only want to be appreciated, they want to feel important.

Making your customers feel important happens when you use their name and go out of your way to provide excellent customer service.

Successful Salespeople over the years have become masterful at not only using a customer's name but also remembering their name.

The next time you interact with a customer, try using their name several times and watch them react positively to your efforts to influence their buying decision.

Finally, make every effort to be likeable with each and every customer and attract your way to success.

Feeling with belief becomes reality

Ten
It's All About Feelings

Succeeding requires assistance from other people. You cannot make any sale without the agreement from your customer to purchase your product or service.

People make decisions and are influenced by their feelings.

"I *felt* very comfortable".

"I had the *feeling* they really wanted my business".

"They made me *feel* like an important customer".

"He was too pushy and I didn't *feel* he was sincere".

"I *felt* like they could take or leave my business".

Customers make decisions based upon the sum total of their feelings. Everything you do and everything you say leaves an impression or a feeling in which the customer comes away with.

The Law of Attraction is powerful but, it works in conjunction with others and attracts, not only things to you, but people as well. This is a key factor in using The Law of Attraction to achieve your goals as a Salesperson.

How you interact with others can and will make a remarkable difference in the final result. Making the sale or not.

The Importance of Importance

Highlighted earlier, every human being alive has the need to feel important. In this chapter, it is the *feeling* that a customer comes away with that deserves our strict attention.

To have your personal worth reaffirmed by others is as important as food and water. It is a universal hunger that each and every one of us needs, craves and requires as a human being.

When we see television advertisements to donate money to help feed the poor we are reminded of the brutal truth that young and old in different parts of the world are in need.

Now, imagine having the power and the financial means to feed every man, woman and child in the world if only for a day. Imagine what good you could do by satisfying the physical needs of those who are much less fortunate than we are.

Physical food is a visible thing. It is something that we can see with our eyes. Conversely, the feeling of importance is not visible. Nevertheless, it is necessary to every person's mental and psychological health.

Whether you realize it or not, you do have the power to affect each and every customer you meet. It is within your power that you have an abundance to help satisfy this human hunger with each and every customer that you encounter. It is within your power to make every single customer you meet to *feel* important.

Give It Away Freely

The most interesting phenomenon that humans demonstrate relative to feelings of importance is that of reciprocity. It can have a positive or a negative influence on human relations.

Reciprocity is the quality of being reciprocal. It is a mutual exchange, mutual action and even mutually influential.

Recently, I stopped into a national chain to grab a breakfast sandwich. The person behind the counter never smiled, never really made eye contact and hardly even acknowledged me as a customer. What was even more surprising was the title under his name tag.

It said, 'General Manager'.

What is even more interesting is that his actions, or lack of, created a reciprocal response from me.

When I climbed back into my vehicle to leave, it struck me that his actions had an impact on me. Due to reciprocity, I adopted his mood. I was influenced by his behavior. And, therefore, I didn't smile back at him or give him any positive energy.

Had the General Manager smiled at me and said, Good Morning, I would have perked up and smiled back. I would have verbalized my enthusiasm in response to his initial positive action. He lost an opportunity to make me feel important and therefore, I left the business establishment actually feeling less important. Reciprocity.

His actions affected my mood.

And, that is the point that cannot be over emphasized. By your words and actions, you interject a certain feeling or mood into your customers.

When you make the customer feel important, you make them feel better about themselves. This is a key element in Sales and is usually the difference maker for top Salespeople.

How To Make Anyone Feel Important

Lack of self-esteem today is an epidemic and, as such, there are countless books on how to elevate self-esteem.

Knowing that many customers lack self-esteem actually creates an opportunity for you to make them *feel* more important. This is not only an advantageous thing to do it is, the right thing to do.

Try these two exercises and test, for yourself, whether this information is true and correct. Once you have seen it first hand and have ownership, you will become a believer and will likely use it to improve your customer interactions.

Walk into any convenience or grocery store and pick out an item to buy and walk over to the check-out counter. Now, the cashier is the person who should initiate positive contact by greeting you and, asking if you found everything you were looking for. However, that does not always happen. The cashier may have had a bad day or they received little sleep the night before. Perhaps, the newborn kept them up most of the night. We really have no idea what challenges others have to deal with and should never take emotional spillover personally.

Nevertheless, as you walk up to pay for your pack of gum, make no effort to initiate any contact. Do not say a word. Give the cashier absolutely no facial expression of any kind.

This experiment provides an opportunity, without any prompting from you, for the cashier to create a positive experience.

Now, please do not misunderstand. This does not mean that you should be rude. Simply give the cashier no energy whatsoever and see what happens.

You should experience this reaction. The cashier is not likely to smile and will not give you much in the way of positive energy. You are likely to walk out of the store without feeling better than you walked in.

Now, travel to a different store and try the opposite approach. As you walk up to pay for your second pack of gum, initiate contact by giving the cashier a big smile and say hello using their name, assuming a name tag is present.

You should experience a different reciprocal reaction from the prior experiment.

This time, the cashier is likely to light up and say something back that is positive. The feeling that you are likely to walk away with is positive and uplifting. That is the reciprocal benefit that you, as a Salesperson, can experience.

One last tip.

While attempting this second experiment, make sure to lift your eyebrows when you say hello to the cashier.

Raising your eyebrows is a signal of recognition and will make your exchange more positive. This technique is critical to making your customer feel important. Using it time and time again will have positive affects as it will give your customer a positive feeling about you and their experience with you.

Make Them Feel Like A Celebrity

The need to *feel* important cannot be overstated. If you make the customer to feel important, you are on your way to creating a great relationship.

How can you ultimately make your customer feel important?

Make them *feel* like a celebrity. Imagine, for a moment, that your favorite actor walked into the room. How would you respond?

How would you react?

No doubt, you would stand up straighter and lift your eyebrows as you gave the actor the recognition and respect you feel that they deserve.

*Having your personal worth affirmed by others
is just as important as food and water*

Now, take that same paradigm and show like recognition and respect to each and every customer that you encounter. Yes, treat them like your favorite celebrity. Get in the habit of imagining that your customer is your favorite actor and you will see a tremendous difference in how they react positively to what you have to say.

The results will astound you as you are giving customers what they really crave, a genuine feeling of importance and recognition.

Feeling important yourself is an attraction factor as you treat each and every person and customer as a celebrity.

The feeling of importance and the fact that you really do have their best interest at heart, that you are truly interested in them personally and not just trying to make the sale will create customer loyalty.

First & Last Words Create Memorable Feelings

Your first and last words with your customer, creates an aggregate *feeling* that stays with them long after your Sales presentation.

Think of the most memorable movies of all time such as, *Gone with the Wind*.

What were the last words Clark Gable spoke to Vivien Leigh as the movie legend walked out?

"Frankly, my dear. I don't give a damn"

Those parting words have been quoted countless times.

Here are some of the top movie quotes to be heard on the big screen. See if you can recall the corresponding movie and the actor:

"Bond, James Bond"

"Of all the gin joints in all the towns in all the world, she walks into mine"

"Well, it's not the men in your life that counts, it's the life in your men"

"I'll be back"

"My Mama always said, Life was like a box of chocolates; you never know what you're gonna get'"

"You talkin' to me?"

Just as the words of any great actor are remembered, customers will remember your words, if and only if, they are truly memorable.

Leaving a customer's home, I once told the woman who had been kind enough to listen to my Sales presentation;

"Thank you for allowing me to come to your home"

I will never forget the look on her face. It was angelic.

It was, as if at that moment, something magical had occurred. With my parting words, I could have been her son who had, at long last, come home from serving in the war.

My words were not scripted, as Clark Gable's were so carefully planned. No, my improvised words just came out of a sincere feeling of appreciation for her being so patient in listening to my presentation. As my last words were unscripted, I really did not expect the reciprocal feeling I received from the customer's smile, as I said goodbye.

Getting back into my car, I immediately wrote down exactly what I had said as I did not want to forget the words that created such feelings. From that point, I made sure that the first and last words of any future Sales presentation would be memorable. Not cheesy or insincere but, genuine.

The overall *feeling* that your customer gets from spending time with you will greatly impact their decision to buy or not to buy your product or service. If you try to make the time they spend with you unforgettable and, if your first and last words are truly memorable then, you will accomplish what many top Salespeople achieve; the ability to separate yourself from the ordinary and subsequently, become elevated to the extraordinary.

Finally, what you personally experience by making the customer to feel important is the reciprocal benefit. The customer, involuntarily, will make you feel equally important and rise to the occasion by giving you the recognition and respect that you deserve.

Actions speak louder than words

Eleven
Body Language

Nonverbal communication or what we know as Body Language often sends a different message than the spoken word.

Research has shown that 90% of all human interaction is nonverbal. Therefore, it's not what is coming out of your mouth that has the most impact upon a customer. It's what your body is revealing that has a far greater influence.

How important is the science of nonverbal communication? In the courtroom and during jury selection, body language experts can be seen studying prospective jurors. They watch what someone does with their face, hands, arms, shoulders and even their eyes and then, interpret what the corresponding body language means.

When a person takes the stand and raises their right hand and says, "I promise to tell the truth, the whole truth and nothing but the truth", the body language expert is looking at their uplifted hand to determine whether the person will actually tell the truth or not.

If the witness has their fingers rigid and wide apart, it reveals that the person is terrified and will likely tell the truth. The mere fact that the fingers are wide apart shows openness and honesty. However, if the fingers are tight together, it says that the witness will tell the truth but it will have to be drawn out of them. Finally, if the hand is bent backward it means that the witness will likely bend over backwards to get the jury to believe them.

Actions do speak louder than words.

Everything you do sends a message. For example, you probably recognize this common body language gesture – when someone has crossed their arms. If you guessed that this person is likely to be defensive, you're right.

However, there is much more to nonverbal communication than understanding when someone has become defensive. In this chapter, you'll learn a number of body language cues that will help you to better understand what customers are most likely to be thinking. This process is called *decoding*. When you have interpreted another person's body language, you have, in effect, decoded what they are thinking or feeling.

Encoding

On the other hand, when you are conscious of how your body language is received by others and you subsequently use specific body language gestures to achieve a favorable response, this is known as *encoding*.

First, let's examine a few body language gestures you can immediately use to greatly improve your success in Sales. These body language cues allow you to create the kind of reaction & positive outcomes you are looking for when interacting with customers. The first one will teach you how to speak so that others will listen.

Holding The Floor

This first body language cue is called *Holding the Floor*. One of the ways you can measure success with customers is how well they listen to you in a conversation. When speaking with others, we sometimes handoff the conversation to the other person to allow them to speak. We do this without even realizing it. It's a common body language cue that says; now it's your turn. However, have you ever felt that the person you were speaking to wasn't listening because they kept interrupting? It can be frustrating when the other person doesn't appear to be interested in what we have to say. So, how can you avoid being interrupted? How can you speak so that customers will listen? The answer is the ability to use the body language gesture called *Holding the Floor*. When you don't want to be interrupted, follow this simple rule; when you are coming to the end of a sentence, break eye contact, allow the person to see you take a quick breath, then return to eye contact and continue speaking.

Many times, people interrupt because we have unintentionally given them a body cue that offers them an opening that says, it's Ok to interrupt. When the other person thinks that you have made your point, they will feel the urge to speak up. If you pause while making continuous eye contact, even just briefly, that pause, is considered a handoff. By mistake, you've sent a body language gesture that says you have passed the discussion to the other person. Inadvertently, you handed the conversation off without even knowing it.

Although it's important to watch body language during any conversation, understanding how to *Hold the Floor* puts you in control and helps you to speak so that customers will listen.

Here's an exercise that will help you master this body language technique. In your next five conversations, practice *Holding The Floor*. If you're not successful in at least three conversations using this technique, come back and review this section again.

Holding the floor is a body language gesture that will help you to be more successful when engaged in a conversation with any customer.

The Confident Voice

The next body language gesture is called, *The Confident Voice.* As previously discussed, speaking with confidence is vital for Salespeople. Customers actually perceive you or value you to the degree that you perceive or value yourself. If you speak with a lack of confidence, how can you expect others to have confidence in you? On a scale of 1 to 10, one being the lowest level of confidence and ten being the highest, if you project confidence at, say a level of seven, can you really expect others to perceive your confidence level at, say a nine or maybe even a ten? The answer is no.

A person will only perceive your confidence to the level that you project.

A person lacking confidence will not project the proper voice tone to create a perception of self-confidence. 38% of communication is the tone of your voice. To project confidence, raise your voice to a level where you feel more confident. At first, you'll feel that you're being too loud, but you're actually not. Here's an exercise that can help you to project *The Confident Voice*. Positioning yourself in front of a mirror, introduce yourself, loudly saying your name over and over until you feel more confident.

Ok, let's give it a try. "Hi, my name is _____, great to meet you. Hi, my name is _____, very nice to meet you. Hi, my name is _____, it's a pleasure to meet you". As you repeat the words, measure yourself on a scale of 1 to 10. Don't stop until you can continuously rate yourself a 10.

Don't underestimate the power of this exercise. Actors seen on TV or in the movies are not born with a confident voice. They practice.

People are influenced to make buying decisions based upon your level of perceived competence, intelligence and ability. As part of The Cues of Influence, *The Confident Voice* along with other body language gestures contained in this chapter can help you to succeed in Sales.

Eye Power

Now, let's examine what is known as *Eye Power*. Just as the tone of your voice can project confidence, direct eye contact communicates to the person you're speaking to, that you are not only confident, you are competent as well.

Maintaining eye contact puts you in control. Another person can tell that you are confident in what you have to say by your ability to maintain eye contact. And, when making a point, holding eye contact says, you know what you're talking about. The eyes are certainly windows to the soul. With our eyes we communicate vast amounts of information. Eye contact demonstrates that you are engaged in the conversation. It says that the other person is important. Making eye contact means that you face them. Turning your body away from someone in conversation shows that you are not truly interested in what they have to say. And, when making a point, direct and continuous eye contact communicates that you have a high degree of self-confidence.

To project confidence, you must avoid excessive eye blinks. If your eyes are blinking more than normal, people are likely to feel that you lack confidence in what you're saying or worse, they may even feel that you are not telling the truth. But, how can you maintain eye contact with someone without being invasive? This is a common dilemma when attempting to maintain eye contact. This brings us to *The Eye Zone*.

The Eye Zone

Understanding *The Eye Zone* can help you maintain eye contact, while allowing the other person to remain comfortable with your gaze.

When you're speaking to someone in conversation, look them directly in the eye.

After you have established eye contact, focus your eyes on the other parts of *The Eye Zone*. Imagine a rectangular square about an inch all the way around their eyes. As you speak to them feel free to move your eyes within *The Eye Zone*. But, remember to rotate between eye contact and other parts of *The Eye Zone*. As an exercise, practice with a family member or a friend to become comfortable using this technique.

Ask them if they feel that you maintained eye contact even though your eyes moved within *The Eye Zone*.

To project confidence, direct eye contact in a conversation is critical. But, making the other person feel comfortable is just as important. By using this technique, others will feel comfortable talking to you. They will appreciate your confidence and will not feel uncomfortable with your gaze.

The Arm Hang

Ever wondered what to do with your hands and arms when engaged in conversation? You're not alone. It's difficult to project confidence when you're hands are in your pockets or worse, when your hands are touching your face.

So, what should you do? The fact is that most people are comfortable when speaking to someone who comes across relaxed and in control.

This brings us to an important body language gesture known as *The Arm Hang*. When engaged in a conversation, just relax and let your arms hang down by your side. It will appear awkward at first, but will feel more natural the more you practice this body cue.

Try this exercise to master *The Arm Hang*. In front of a mirror, stand erect and let your arms hang in a relaxed manner. Imagine you're in a conversation with someone that otherwise might be intimidating to you, like your boss or perhaps the person you're giving a Sales presentation. Once you've become completely relaxed, notice how your arms are hanging. Practice this exercise every day for five days. The arm hang can help you appear more confident in any business situation.

Power Positions

Have you ever noticed that in the courtroom, the Judge is seated higher than anyone else? That is no accident. In the world of nonverbal communication, it is what is called a position of power. By being seated higher than anyone else, the Judge has taken a *Power Position*.

In virtually every business setting, you have opportunities to assume a dominant role or a *Power Position*.

This does not mean that you should dominate your customer. It simply means that the person seated highest will tip the position of power to their side while likely boosting their confidence.

Here's an example. If you will be conducting a sales presentation, think ahead as to where it will take place. Think of the environment and how you can arrange a *Power Position*. If it's not possible to prearrange your meeting, many chairs, especially in conference rooms have an adjustment just below the chair on the right hand side. Before you begin your presentation or meeting, adjust your chair to its highest level. This will create a position of power that will boost your self-confidence and help you to deliver a better presentation or conduct a more successful meeting.

The Curse of the Sunken Chest

There is no question that body posture plays a key role in your success. Customers are influenced to make decisions based upon how they perceive the person they are dealing with. People want to interact with those who they believe to be capable, smart, energetic and enthusiastic. Let's take a moment and imagine two different kinds of Salespeople. You decide which one appears to be more capable. The first has excellent posture and stands erect. Next, imagine a Salesperson who is standing with their shoulders slumped forward.

Having these two mental pictures in mind, it's not hard, therefore, to decide which of these two Salespeople you would rather do business with.

You decide which one appears to be more intelligent and more confident.

You decide which person you would prefer to deal with. Imagine a Salesperson who stands erect with shoulders back and

The Salesperson with poor body posture is suffering from *The Curse of the Sunken Chest*. Their shoulders are slumped forward and the chest is nowhere to be found. It's as if their chest has been dropped off the side of a ship and has been lost in the watery depths below, gone forever.

Would you have confidence in this Salesperson? Probably not. Would you perceive this person to be capable of handling your account or business?

Again, probably not.

Now, let's examine the person who projected the correct body posture. Notice that they appear to be more confident, energetic, enthusiastic and certainly more capable. This is certainly the type of person that anyone would rather purchase a product or service from.

Try this exercise. Standing in front of a mirror, take a few moments to just stand with an upright and erect body posture. In a few seconds, you'll feel more confident and successful. More importantly, you'll appear to be more capable, more intelligent, enthusiastic and energetic. Practice this exercise once a day for five days. Moving forward, customers will notice the difference in your upright and erect body posture. Learning to master this body language gesture can help you in your quest for success in Sales.

The Eyebrow Flash

This point bears repeating. Everyone you wish to do business with wants to be recognized as a valued customer. If you've ever been shopping and, encountered a Salesperson that didn't show much interest in you as a potential customer, you understand how it feels not to be recognized.

When greeting a customer, there are many different words to use to express the fact that you welcome their business and that you value them as a customer, however, words cannot replace the body language gesture known as *The Eyebrow Flash*.

The Eyebrow Flash is an up and down movement of the eyebrows. When greeting someone and while making initial eye contact, raise your eyebrows. It lasts for a brief moment and is used only when making initial eye contact. It may seem a little childish to be raising your eyebrows like a cartoon character. But, with a little practice, it'll feel completely natural. Try this exercise. When greeting the next person you come in contact with, raise your eyebrows up and down. Measure their reaction. Then, with the next person leave out the eyebrow flash. You will notice the customer you gave an eyebrow flash to was more open and easier to do business with.

The Eyebrow Flash is a gesture of recognition. It says, I appreciate you, I like you, and I accept you. People want to feel important. *The Eyebrow Flash* says to your customer, that they are important.

To be successful, you must be perceived by others as likeable, therefore, when greeting people, make sure to include *The Eyebrow Flash*.

The Head Nod

There is nothing that communicates to the person you're speaking to that says you're interested in what they have to say like *The Head Nod*. Nodding your head when listening to a customer, says to them that you understand their concerns or requests. Now, let's discuss two different types of head nods. The slow head nod and the fast.

The slow head nod communicates that you are listening intently. It says you are carefully considering what the other person has to say. On the other hand, nodding the head fast can be interpreted to mean that you are not listening. This can be especially true if there is little to no eye contact or if you are blinking your eyes excessively. However, there is a place for the faster head nod. After listening to the other person and you feel the other person wants to turn the conversation over to you, begin to nod your head slightly faster than before. This will signal that, after you have heard them out, you're ready to take over the conversation.

So, when listening to someone either in a business setting, slowly nod your head as you listen and focus on what the customer is saying.

The Mighty Pen

As we have seen, people have an intrinsic need to be recognized. When someone takes a special interest in us personally, we feel better about ourselves. We like ourselves more.

In Sales, you have the opportunity to fulfill this most basic human need by writing down what a customer says. Smart Salespeople use a notebook or a simple notepad to write down the customer's wants and needs. When a customer sees you writing down what their specific requirements are, they gain a sense of self-importance.

The Mighty Pen is a way to communicate nonverbally that the customer is important and you value their business. Without saying a word, the customer will feel better about the total buying experience and will more than likely tell others about your products and services.

To learn more about these body language techniques, there are two videos that can help you to master the art of nonverbal communication. *Success and Confidence for Men* and *Success and Confidence for Women* are available for purchase. Visit; www.InterSkillMedia.com

Decoding Body Language

Now that we have covered the importance of encoding body language cues that will help create a positive response with customers, let's discuss decoding body language gestures.

Understanding a customer's body language can help you to understand what they are thinking and absolutely establishes a communication advantage.

The Evaluation Cue

Customers will show you a sign demonstrating that they are seriously considering what you are saying. When speaking to a customer who is stroking their chin, they are demonstrating the body language gesture known as *The Evaluation Cue*.

This body cue is very easy to recognize and interpret. The customer who expresses this body language cue is likely to be interested in what you have to say. Of course, if the customer has a frown on their face as they stroke their chin, then the customer is giving a negative evaluation to what they are hearing.

At this point, you should recall the previous words you have just said and ask the customer what they may have a concern with or perhaps they have a question that needs to be addressed.

The mistake many Salespeople make is to completely ignore their customer's body language and continue on with the sale, or worse, try to close the sale too soon. When a customer demonstrates *The Evaluation Cue* more questions need to be asked. As you ask the customer more detailed questions, observe their body language and respond accordingly.

The Steeple

Customers can easily become confident in their opinions or decisions. A common body language cue you should look for is *The Steeple*.

This body language cue is revealed when a customer puts their hands together with only the tips of their fingers touching and looks exactly like a church steeple.

The Steeple is always connected with a sense of confidence. If a customer displays *The Steeple* gesture at chest level, it usually indicates that they are confident about what they are saying, however, if the gesture is displayed at lap level it usually indicates that they are confident in what they are hearing.

Just as a sentence contains a group of words put together, body language works in the same manner. When the customer is displaying *The Steeple* and you recognize the gesture correctly as a sign of confidence, it's important to recall what particular body language gesture preceded *The Steeple*.

If the customer displayed positive body language prior to *The Steeple*, then you could correctly conclude that the customer is likely to do business with you. However, if the customer displayed negative body language prior to *The Steeple* such as looking at their watch, breaking eye contact or a critical evaluation gesture such as resting their hand on the side of their face with their index finger pointed toward their head, then you must conclude that the customer is not in agreement with you and unless a different approach is taken, will typically choose not do business with you.

The Doubting Thomas

During a conversation, a person may demonstrate a body language gesture that expresses doubt or a lack of self-confidence. This common body cue is called *The Doubting Thomas*.

When a person expresses doubt or even deceit, they will begin to rub one of their eyebrows with their left hand. When a person begins to rub their eyebrow, it is obvious that they are not comfortable answering a particular question or they are expressing doubt in what they are hearing.

It is also possible that when someone feels that their words are not likely to be believed, they will also demonstrate *The Doubting Thomas* gesture.

As you engage in conversations with others, watch for *The Doubting Thomas* body language gesture as it will reveal what your customer is thinking or feeling.

The Crossed Arm

Most Salespeople have the ability to decode *The Crossed Arm*. This body language cue is usually understood to mean that a customer has become defensive. However, knowing what this body language gesture means and dealing with it is another matter.

To correctly interpret this body language cue, it would be wise to consider what their facial expression is saying.

Does the customer appear to be upset?

If so, their fingers are likely to be pressed into their arms and will not appear to be relaxed. How can you deal with this type of body language? Ask! Yes, ask the customer if they have any questions or concerns that you may not have covered. You may be surprised to learn that the issue has nothing to do with you or your product or service. Conversely, when a customer has crossed their arms, it does not always indicate that the customer has become defensive.

Many customers cross their arms when listening or relaxing. Crossing the arms is also called a Coaches Position when the person is relaxed and their fingers are wide apart. When a woman crosses her arms, it can simply indicate that she is cold or simply uncomfortable. You should then ask if she is cold. If she says she is not, then ask if any additional questions or concerns need to be addressed. What must be understood when a customer has crossed their arms is the fact that they are mentally closed

Many Salespeople completely ignore their customer's body language off and are likely to resist change or closed off to receiving new information, ideas or concepts.

The goal, when encountering any customer who has crossed their arms, is simply a matter of getting them *uncrossed*. You can accomplish this by handing them something to read such as a brochure and then sharing with them the information that will help you move on to closing the sale.

The Tilted Head

When a person begins to tilt their head, you should immediately recall the words or ideas you have just expressed. *The Tilted Head* is a body language gesture that reveals interest. When a person is showing interest, they will tilt their head and perhaps begin to lean in. Always observe your customer's body language and continually guage their level of interest. When a person begins to tilt their head, you probably need to either ask them to make a decision or move on toward closing the sale.

Lying or deceit

In any situation, we depend on others to be truthful with their expressions regarding their wants and needs. However, because some customers want the advantage to tip in their favor, they are not always honest. Your ability to determine when a person is being truthful can certainly aid to your success in Sales. Body language experts specialize in indicating when someone is telling the truth or when someone is telling a lie. The research shows many different body language gestures reveal when someone is not telling the truth. Here are several body language gestures you can look for when dealing with a customer.

First, anytime a person is uncomfortable with a particular subject they will break eye contact and subsequently touch their face, slightly rub their nose or eyebrow. How can you be sure your interpretation is correct?

If you feel that the person is being less than truthful with you, come back in two to three minutes and ask them another question on the same subject and carefully take note of their body language. If the person displays the same behavior that originally made you uncomfortable, uneasy or concerned then, your initial impression was correct. This person is lying.

Another technique that can give you an advantage is to use an open hand gesture when dealing with customers. If your hands are open, it will usually help to suppress any dishonesty on the part of the person you are dealing with.

Never jump to the conclusion that a customer may be lying to you, however, test your feelings and address the subject again and see if the same body language is displayed a second or even a third time.

Micro Expressions

As we've seen in this chapter, most all body language occurs at a speed that is visible to the naked eye allowing the opportunity to Encode and Decode nonverbal communication. There is, however, another element of nonverbal communication that deserves attention. It is called, *Micro Expressions*. A *Micro Expression* is a body language gesture that occurs so rapidly that it is difficult for the naked eye to see it.

Most women are much better at reading body language than men.

However, even with the superior ability to decode body language, a *Micro Expression* occurs so quickly that even the naked eye of a female rarely sees it. However, with Micro Expressions, a female will receive a composite positive or negative feeling from these *Micro Expressions*.

Here is a fun exercise and one that demonstrates how difficult *Micro Expressions* can be for anyone to detect, male or female.

In the movie *Hitch*, starring Will Smith, Eva Mendes and Kevin James, a particular scene in the film beautifully demonstrates a series of *Micro Expressions*.

In this scene, Will Smith sees Eva Mendes in a nightclub and wants to meet her. He strikes up a conversation with the bartender who says that she's a regular and a good tipper. The bartender mixes her favorite cocktail, a Grey Goose Martini. Will Smith takes the two drinks, one for himself of course, over to Eva but, before he gets there another would-be-suitor named Chip beats him to the punch.

Will listens to Chip attempt, unsuccessfully I might add, to woo the beautiful Eva Mendes. Here is where our lesson on *Micro Expressions* begins.

But, wait! Before you read on, rent the movie and watch this particular scene all the way through without stopping.

Alright, if you've watched the scene, keep reading.

Now, after Chip is spurned by Eva, ask yourself these two important questions:

What is your impression of Chip? Do you like or dislike him?

Now, write down in the spaces provided below the reason(s) you like him or dislike him.

_____

_____

_____

_____

Alright, you now have an impression of Chip. Watch it again and go through the scene, frame by frame and break it down in order for you to better understand what *Micro Expressions* are and how difficult they can be to detect. You will want to take your TV or DVD remote to freeze each frame or to stop frame to frame so that you can observe each *Micro Expression*. With the initial frames of the scene, Chip has a *frown* on his face when he says, "Hi." Then, he proceeds to show his *tongue* which is not a great way to make a first impression with a lady. These two micro expressions would make any female uncomfortable.

Next, Chip sits down uninvited and is *elevated* above her and by doing so, takes a *dominant position*. This is not a positive body language gesture. He then proceeds to *rub his hands* together which can easily be perceived as an *expectation* gesture. Too much expectation if you ask the average female. He also sits the drink down with his fingers on the outside of the glass where she would put her lips to take a drink.

Not a smart thing to do for someone who is trying to make a memorable first impression. Finally, Chip *stares* at her chest for a full seven frames, long enough for any female to feel uncomfortable with this stranger.

The benefit of actually seeing these *Micro Expressions* one-by-one and especially after watching this particular scene and missing them the first time through is invaluable. Of course, watching the scene initially gave you an accumulative feeling about Chip even without seeing the individual *Micro Expressions*. Finally, watching the scene again frame by frame brought your feelings to a reality as you were able to identify the source of your feelings.

What can we learn from this form of nonverbal communication?

Trust your feelings. Yes, listen to what your intuition is telling you. The *Micro Expressions* that a person puts off may be difficult to decode, however, you will feel their impact resulting in an overall feeling about the person.

Research shows that 90% of all communication is nonverbal or what we have come to recognize from this chapter as, *body language gestures.*

Start immediately to implement your newfound knowledge with all your business contacts, presentations, or during everyday conversation.

You will find that exploring body language is not only a learned skill, it is a fascinating journey.

An obstacle is an opportunity in disguise

Twelve
Obstacles

Success and obstacles go together like salt and pepper. It's hard to have one without the other. Whatever your dream, desire or goal, it will come only after you have endured a series of obstacles that impedes or perhaps slows down your progress.

For many, a series of obstacles will cause an eventual give up mentality and soon after, the dream, desire or goal eventually fades into a distant memory.

The secret to overcoming obstacles is to understand their value and how to deal with them.

An obstacle is not an enemy. It is your best friend. The vast majority of people think that failure should be avoided at all cost. Much of what is seen on TV and in the movies generally glamorizes success while at the same time minimizing the importance of failure.

Failure is the secret to success. It is certainly through failure that the following individuals ultimately achieved success.

The Story of Milton Hershey

Milton Hershey, the founder of the famous chocolate bar bearing his name, was born in 1857.

Milton's father, Henry, had an entrepreneurial spirit but, many of his speculative endeavors to earn a living ended in failure. Despite his father's poor track record, Milton was not discouraged.

At the age of 14, *(opportunity)* Milton was apprenticed in a local print shop but, *(obstacle)* was dismissed for lack of attention to the trade. In 1872, shortly after the failed printing apprenticeship, his mother arranged for Milton to be apprenticed to a Lancaster confectionery shop making candy. *(opportunity)* He enjoyed it so much that his enthusiasm and skill led him to launch his own candy business.

At 19, *(opportunity)* Milton established his first business venture in Philadelphia. His mother and her sister provided the financial support needed to launch the business. In spite of the help from his family and friends, *(obstacle)* Milton was forced to declare bankruptcy.

After the business failed, Milton joined his father in Colorado *(opportunity)* where Henry had hopes of striking it rich in the silver mines. But, *(obstacle)* Henry arrived too late and once again was jobless. However, he managed to find a job *(opportunity)* with a candy maker where he learned many vital lessons to making great tasting candy, most of which was the value of using fresh milk.

In 1883, *(opportunity)* Milton launched a second venture into the candy business in New York City. Unfortunately, *(obstacle)* with little capital and severe competition, the business collapsed.

At the age of 29, Milton returned to his family home in Lancaster, only to be shunned *(obstacle)* by his uncles who had suffered the loss of their investment in his failed business ventures. He was looked upon as being as financially irresponsible as his father, Henry Hershey.

Vowing not to give up *(persistence)* and with another loan from his aunt, *(opportunity)* he was able to purchase the ingredients to begin a caramel making business. He made his candy by day, and sold it in the evening using a pushcart. Soon, *(opportunity)* an English importer of candy, greatly impressed with the fresh taste and quality of the caramels, gave Milton a huge order of candy. Obtaining a loan from a bank, Milton was able to fill the Englishman's order. The large order was filled and made him enough money to pay off the bank loan and launch a successful caramel-making business.

Four years after his failures in Philadelphia and New York, Milton Hershey became a successful businessman and a millionaire. *(success!)*

The Story of Colonel Sanders

Harland Sanders was born in 1890 in Indiana. His father died *(obstacle)* when he was only 6 years old which left him as the man of the house with a mother, a brother and a sister. Sanders *(opportunity)* picked up the art of cooking quickly and mastered many dishes by the age of 7. In his early years, Sanders worked odd jobs to help support the family. He was a farm-hand, streetcar conductor, soldier, fireman, self-taught lawyer, insurance Salesman, and a steamboat operator. At the age of 40, *(opportunity)* he was cooking for travelers out of a gas station. Word of his delicious cooking spread and soon there were huge lines for his food causing him to move his business across the street to a motel and restaurant to service the demand. Sanders *(opportunity)* began to experiment with his special herbs and spices to make what many know today as his trademark 11 herbs and spices.

In 1950 at the age of 60, Sanders had to shut down his business *(obstacle)* due to a new highway being built right where his restaurant was located.

Finally, Sanders decided it was time to retire. It wasn't long before Sanders grew tired of retirement and *(opportunity)* decided to franchise his chicken recipe. So, he began to travel by car to different restaurants and cooked his fried chicken on the spot for restaurant owners. If the owner liked the chicken, they would enter into a handshake agreement to sell the Colonel's chicken. Attempting to franchise his recipe, *(obstacle)* Sanders heard more than 1,000 *no's* before he heard even one *yes*. Imagine. Colonel Sanders was turned down more than 1,000 times before the first restaurant accepted his offer!

And, what was the offer?

For each piece of chicken the restaurant sold, Sanders would receive a nickel. In exchange, the restaurant purchased packets of Colonel's secret herbs and spices in order to avoid them knowing the recipe. By 1964 and *(persistence)* after not giving up, Colonel Sanders had 600 franchises selling his trademark chicken. At this time, he sold his company for $2 million dollars but, remained as a spokesperson. In 1976, the Colonel was ranked as the world's second most recognizable celebrity. *(success!)*

The Inventor of the Light Bulb

Thomas Edison faced many *obstacles* as an inventor. He had a creative mind that was ready for one experiment after the other. Many of them, like the light bulb, the phonograph, and the motion picture camera, were brilliant inventions. However, not everything he created was an immediate success; he had many *obstacles* to overcome. He made over 1,000 unsuccessful attempts at inventing the light bulb. When a reporter asked how it felt to fail so many times, Edison said the light bulb was an invention with 1,000 steps. He completely understood the process of invention. Edison learned that *obstacles* lead to *success.*

Understanding Obstacles

The dictionary defines an obstacle as something that impedes progress when one is working toward a goal. In Sales and in business, that definition is only part of the story. Each and every Salesperson must contend with a multitude of challenges.

An obstacle is like a traffic light. It can temporarily halt or even slow your progress, but is not permanent. How you perceive obstacles as either temporary or permanent will make the difference when you are striving to achieve success in Sales.

Imagine pulling up to a stop sign and the driver ahead of you is out of his car, sitting on the trunk with his head in his hands, completely dejected. You ask him what is wrong. He says that everything was going great until he had to stop at this four way stop. He explains that not only was he not prepared for the stop sign, he has no idea whether he should go straight ahead, turn left or right.

In Sales, many find themselves in this same predicament. Obstacles get in the way, slow them down or cause them to stop altogether.

The question really is a matter of understanding how obstacles help you refine your goal or even present an opportunity that you were not even aware of.

The Story of the Sticky Note Pad

Most everyone today has used a sticky note pad. They are great little self sticking notepapers that help you stay organized and come in many colors including, pink, yellow and green. Many people really love them and could not do without them. However, the sticky note pad was not a product that was preplanned. It was discovered by means of an *obstacle*.

In a 3M research laboratory in the early 1970's, a man by the name of Spencer Silver was attempting to find a strong adhesive. Unfortunately, the new adhesive he developed was even weaker than what 3M had already produced. Sure enough, his new adhesive would stick to objects but, could be easily pulled off. Not exactly what he was trying to achieve for 3M.

Several years later, another 3M scientist named Arthur Fry was singing in a church choir when his markers kept falling out of his song book. Remembering Silver's adhesive, Fry used some of the weak adhesive on his markers to keep them in place. It was a *success*. The weak adhesive kept his markers in place and also lifted off without tearing or damaging the page.

In 1980, 3M began distributing the sticky note pads with the weak adhesive and today has become one of the most popular office products available.

A Valuable Lesson

This story provides a valuable lesson in understanding *failure* and overcoming *obstacles*. When Silver discovered that the new adhesive was weak instead of the optimum strength, he deemed the new adhesive a failure but, not a complete failure.

The genius was *not* discarding the weaker adhesive and, therefore, treating it as a complete failure. The weaker adhesive was still available several years later when Fry saw a door of opportunity. When confronted with an *obstacle*, treating it as an *opportunity* can help you achieve your goal or purpose.

For example, if your goal was to make a certain amount of money, do you really care how you achieved it, provided it was acquired ethically, morally and legally? Of, course not.

What is the ultimate goal or purpose of a company like 3M? Is it not creating products that generate revenue for the company while benefiting the lives and businesses of its customers? Of, course. Does the company care what the product is or does as long as it is a safe product and generates Sales? Of, course not.

That is the difference in *Plan vs Purpose* as we discussed in Chapter 2. When you purpose something, you are not unduly concerned when things do not work out as planned. You understand what you have purposed and you work toward it while being completely open to any *obstacle* that comes along. Doing so keeps your mind open to new opportunities and The Law of Attraction can help you to achieve your goal or purpose.

Viewing an *obstacle* as an ally and not an enemy is actually part of the process in achieving your objectives.

Many get upset when things do not work out precisely as they had planned but, knowing when to make lemonade out of lemons is a secret to success and a key component to The Law of Attraction. When one door closes, many doors will open *if* your mind's eye can perceive them.

Now, let's go back to the figurative stop sign. Imagine that you are driving down a narrow two lane road and to your left is an expressway you would prefer to be on. You have an appointment and you wish not to be late. The expressway, in your mind, would allow you to get to your appointment on time. Now, it's just a matter of how you will get on the expressway. Driving along, you come to a four way stop on the narrow two lane road. You could become frustrated at having to stop. You could behave as the earlier example of the driver who was found sitting on the trunk of his car dejected. That may sound ridiculous however, Salespeople every day stop when facing obstacles that impede their progress. Instead, your positive mind-set allows you to see a possible opportunity by turning left. Perhaps, the road to the left will take you to an on-ramp to the expressway. Turning left, you go under the expressway and it quickly becomes obvious that turning left was not the answer. As you return to the four-way stop, you decide to head in the direction you originally intended. But, before turning left, you see a bridge that leads to the expressway. Energized, you drive straight ahead or from the original position at the four-way stop you're actually turning right and in minutes find the expressway that takes you to the appointment and on time.

Sometimes plowing straight ahead is not always the best answer. When you face an *obstacle*, try to examine what you are actually dealing with. Don't stop until you figure out how you can overcome it. Look for doors of *opportunity* that will lead you to your goal or purpose. There will be doors of opportunity, if and only if, you keep looking.

Accidents Happen

What we know today as the potato chip was invented by a chef. But, the potato chip was not invented because he was trying to create a new type of food.

They were invented because the chef *(obstacle)* was tired of listening to one of his customers who constantly complained. One of his customers kept on sending back his plate of potatoes, complaining *(failure)* that they weren't thin enough or fried long enough. In response, the chef sliced the potatoes razor-thin and fried them longer than he ever had before, sending them back to the customer. To his surprise, the customer loved them *(opportunity)* and the potato chip was born. *(success!)*

Some of the best inventions were created merely by accident. Like the potato chip, the pop-cycle, coca-cola and many more came about due to perceived failure. If the

View each obstacle as an ally

chef had not been paying attention, who knows, a company called Frito Lay may never have existed if not for the accidental potato chip.

Your product or service certainly has its current use as well as its value. However, continually look for opportunities where your product or service can be utilized for other purposes.

Doors of Opportunity

The Law of Attraction is at work, with or without you. If you make a purchase or are thinking of buying something, you will frequently see that same item as in the earlier example of the new vehicle purchase.

However, if you were not interested in that item does that mean that the item then does not exist or, are you just not seeing it?

Allowing the principles of The Law of Attraction to have an influence in the achievement of your desires creates doors of opportunity. Each door is unique.

One is an *obstacle* while the next is an *accident*.

The secret to benefiting from The Law of Attraction is to never allow your mind to discourage you or talk you out of moving forward toward your goal. Your dream, along with your desires, can be achieved by continuing to turn over more rocks in the quarry of success.

There are many examples of people in modern times that have overcome tremendous obstacles.

Oprah Winfrey is among that list.

Oprah Gail Winfrey was born in 1954 and is often referred to simply as Oprah. She is an American television host, a media mogul, and a generous philanthropist. Her internationally-syndicated talk show, The Oprah Winfrey Show, has earned her multiple Emmy Awards and is one of the highest-rated talk shows in the history of television. Oprah Winfrey has also become an influential book critic, an Academy Award-nominated actress, and a magazine publisher. To many, she has also become one of the world's most influential women.

Oprah was born in rural Mississippi to a poor unwed mother in her teens. She grew up in an inner city neighborhood in Milwaukee. At the age of nine she was raped and, later at fourteen, she gave birth to a son who died in infancy. Afterward, she was sent to live with the man she calls her father, a barber in Tennessee. Winfrey landed a job in radio while still in high school and began co-anchoring the local evening news at the age of 19. Her emotional, as well as her spontaneous delivery, eventually landed her on a daytime talk show. And, after boosting a local Chicago talk show from third place to first, she launched her own production company.

In addition to her philanthropy, Oprah is admired by her loyal audience for her ability to successfully deal with adversity.

She overcame many obstacles in the achievement of her dreams. Her example provides hope that anyone can overcome insurmountable odds if one does not allow obstacles to defeat them in the pursuit of their dreams.

People Want Your Product or Service

Whether you are just getting started in Sales or have years of experience, there are people who have a need for your product or service or a version of it. When you follow the principles of The Law of Attraction, these prospective customers and the doors of opportunity that lead you to them will become manifest.

However, you must focus on your goals and work back to the present. Never lose sight of the fact that your product or service is only a means to an end.

Unfortunately, many Salespeople try to increase their Sales by solely focusing on their product or service. This activity can be compared to driving on square wheels rather than round. This is not The Law of Attraction. Starting with your ultimate goal, dream or desire first, will bring you to the present and will help you determine what you need to accomplish *with* your product or service in order to achieve your goal. This process will allow you to successfully deal with obstacles.

Let's explore that subject for a moment. Imagine you are selling a product or service that is extremely competitive. Of course, what isn't competitive today? Everything seems to be extremely competitive! However, many products and services have become commodities. With every product or service you will find those who have no marketing skills and no imagination whatsoever. The only way these companies or individual Salespeople are able to increase Sales is to lower the price in order for them to be competitive. If this describes your competitive landscape, you have my sincerest sympathies.

With extreme competition in mind, let me take you back to the late 1980's to the world of the automotive aftermarket parts industry. No one in that industry would argue the fact that the automotive aftermarket parts industry is extremely competitive. It is a brutal and fiercely competitive market.

In the late 1980's, the Environmental Protection Agency, or EPA, sought to ban asbestos in automobile brake linings. Asbestos brake linings were inexpensive at the time with certain vehicle part numbers selling wholesale for as little as $4 to $5 per vehicle. The asbestos brake linings had become a commodity.

At the same time, front wheel drive vehicles were becoming more prevalent in the late 1980's. However, the heat generated by the front rotors of these front wheel drive vehicles made asbestos linings ineffective. Therefore, metallic brake linings were introduced to handle the heat so that a vehicle could stop more effectively. However, it didn't take unimaginative companies and their brainless Salespeople to turn the new metallic brake lining also into a commodity. Their packaging was plain and their prices were low and many customers, in an effort to save money, purchased them.

If you were in that business, how would you have handled that *obstacle*?

The door of opportunity presented itself with a brake lining made with Kevlar. It was non-asbestos and non-metallic. This product was an excellent product and solved many problems for automotive technicians who were seeking a solution.

How then could anyone sell against low prices whether the competition was selling asbestos or non-asbestos? Again, that was the obstacle. Yet, customers wanted and were willing to pay for a good product.

The answer came with the problems asbestos and metallic brake linings were associated with. Asbestos was not effective or applicable on all vehicles and metallic brake linings created dusty and dirty wheels that made many vehicles unattractive. Metallic brake linings were also noisy. They inherently squealed and if the car windows were rolled down, the metallic brake linings could make any driver insane from the relentless noise.

Automobile repair centers knew of these problems and were ready for an answer. So, the new non-asbestos and non-metallic Kevlar brake linings were sold in great numbers and at above average prices. The packaging was first rate, not a plain white box but a bright red colorful box along with incentives for using the product. The new brake linings were successful because they solved a problem automotive technicians want to resolve.

How can you use that example in your industry? People want your product or service or a version of it. Ask yourself what are the challenges your customers face? What problems can your product or service solve?

Necessity is the mother of invention or, as we have seen earlier, obstacles as well as accidents create opportunities. The tendency is to overlook opportunities. Why? Because, most of the time we're not forced to. We get comfortable with the status quo. Why make things hard when life is easy?

The beauty of the Law of Attraction is that it creates opportunity. When you become totally focused on your goal, dream or desire, your eyes will see doors of opportunity opening to you. You will begin to see what you did not see before.

The more intense the desire to achieve your goal is and the more specific your goal, the greater your success will be in dealing with obstacles. When your goal dominants your thoughts, you will become obsessed with finding a way to make it a reality. This is The Law of Attraction at work.

In your quest to realize your dreams, you will no doubt encounter many obstacles. Use each one to spur you on to success. Despite conventional thinking, learn from your experiences and never view failure as the end but, only the beginning.

The Law of Attraction is powerful. With a positive attitude and a healthy view of obstacles, you can overcome each and every challenge.

See each obstacle, not as a set-back but, as a learning experience.

Take something away from each failure and use what you have learned to motivate you to keep moving forward.

Doing so will help you to keep pressing on until you have achieved success.

We are all individuals

Thirteen
Respecting Individuality

The fingerprint is an amazing part of the human anatomy. It represents a person's very own individuality. Our fingerprint is unique. No two of the more than 6 billion on the earth are alike.

Little did anyone know 150 years ago that law enforcement officials today would use finger print technology to catch someone guilty of committing a serious crime. In 1892, Juan Vucetich, an Argentine police officer who had been studying the concept of fingerprinting, made one of the first criminal fingerprint identifications. He was able to successfully prove that Francisca Rojas was guilty of murder after showing that the bloody fingerprint Vucetich found at the crime scene belonged to Rojas, and no one else.

Actually, finger print technology was invented simply by accident. A glass container in a laboratory was cracked and powerful glue was used to seal the crack and hold the glass in place. The next day, the glass was still in place but the glue revealed obvious fingerprints on the glass and the world of fingerprinting began.

Looking Through Their Eyes

Just as each fingerprint is unique, so too are each and every customer you meet. Each one has their own personal tastes, likes and dislikes. Acknowledging and respecting a customer's individuality is a necessary component to achieving success in Sales.

Not acknowledging this success principle is one of the primary reasons why many Salespeople rarely achieve extraordinary results. In Sales, focusing only on what you like or dislike is a dangerous and narrow minded approach. If you talk only about what you are enthused about instead of asking the customer what he or she really wants then, success and its monetary benefits will elude you.

Your customers have their very own unique wants, needs and desires. Sometimes, it is difficult for them to express exactly what it is they're after. Time and patience on your part will ultimately make the difference.

Value Systems

A Salesperson I was acquainted with had spent his first two weeks in Sales and, afterward, he called to let me know he was going to quit. I asked him why. He said he could not expect his customers to pay full retail when he would never do so himself. The company he worked for negotiated prices but was obviously interested in getting the full retail price whenever possible. He said he felt that he was cheating a customer when asking them to pay the retail price.

After I listened to his explanation, I asked him to tell me his favorite color. He then asked what that had to do with his leaving the company. I told him that it had everything to do with his giving up.

He said that, if he had to choose, it would be blue and red. He liked both and couldn't decide on only one. I then asked him if he expected every customer that came in to purchase any of the products he sold to choose blue or red. He said, of course not. Everyone has their favorite color, he said. Then, I asked him how he could expect everyone to purchase a product the very same way he did with the intent on negotiating the price down to a level only he was comfortable with.

I think he got the point. Everyone purchases products differently. Some like to make quick decisions and get on with life. Others like to take their time. Some like to negotiate while others grant the Salesperson the opportunity to justify the retail price.

Moreover, what one customer perceives to be a priority, another has no interest or what one perceives as value, another sees as waste.

Recently, I was driving to work one morning. Stopping at a traffic light I looked over and noticed a set of brand new shiny wheels under the car next to me. Admiring the expensive wheels, my attention then turned to the vehicle itself. To my surprise, the wheels must have cost two to three times what the entire car was worth. I then produced a half smile thinking to myself what a waste this young man behind the wheel had made. My initial reaction told me the money had been spent foolishly due to the fact that I would never make such a poor decision myself. Obviously, it made me feel better about myself to make such an assessment.

Then, the voice of reason took over. As I still had my head turned toward the twenty year old vehicle with the new shiny wheels, I realized the mistake and the erroneous judgment I had just rendered.

What I thought was a waste of money was based upon my value system. My opinion was based upon my set of standards.

Staring down at the shiny wheels, sensibility rose to the occasion as I thought to myself, who am I to judge another person's system of values? As the light turned green and the old car lurched forward, I looked upon the young man in a whole new light. It was his choice whether or not to spend more on his wheels than on his entire vehicle.

And, therein is the challenge to achieving success in the world of Sales. Continuing to impose your own value system upon your customer will forever be to your financial detriment. This is a principle that cannot be ignored. Conversely, allowing your customer the freedom to be themselves is one of the success secrets that will move you forward toward achieving your goals and dreams.

Looking through your customer's eyes takes great patience and exceptional listening skills.

However, once you have identified what the customer really wants and then provide them with the product or service that fills their needs can make you very successful.

Never Assume Anything

A very good friend of mine once told a story that demonstrates that you can never assume anything regarding customers. His favorite story occurred when he was working at a retail store and on a particular Monday overheard some of the Salespeople talking about what had happened the previous Saturday.

It seems a farmer came into the showroom and began to look at the brand new products displayed in all their glory. He didn't appear to be very prosperous as his clothes were dirty, torn and ragged. As the story goes, the man waited in the showroom for more than half an hour while none of the Salespeople approached him. To them, he looked too poor to afford any item in the store and appeared to be a complete waste of their time.

Finally, the poor man went to the receptionist and asked to see the Manager. The Sales Manager came out and, never turning down a customer, helped the farmer purchase one of the new products on display. The item was paid with cash. As you can imagine, the Sales meeting the next Monday focused on, as you would imagine, never prejudge a customer. You can never tell who will buy and who is merely looking. You may think you know but, you really don't. The only person you're fooling is yourself. So, treat every customer as if they could afford the purchase. If not today, likely it will happen in the future. Never pass up an opportunity to help someone even though a commission isn't likely. You never know who you are really dealing with and you don't know what the future will bring. That customer will need other products and services in the future.

Your Way Is Not The Only Way

While individuality is the fragrance of life, presuming that everyone thinks or even behaves the way we do is the disgusting odor of failure.

Human nature causes each and every one of us to look through our own filter. Each experience we have in Sales as well as in life molds our belief system and creates a filter all our own. Our filter creates a strong bias that can easily be imposed upon another. Based upon your experience, a certain product, color or feature might be, in your mind, a waste of money or vice versa. On the other hand, your own experience may dictate that a certain product, color or feature is best. However, imposing your value system or belief system on your customer is very shortsighted and detrimental to your success in Sales.

Instead of making the customer experience difficult, the experience can and should be fun and enjoyable if you allow the customer to express their own individuality. Continue to resist the urge to impose your value or belief system upon your customer and reap the positive results.

'The Power of 3'

Energy and enthusiasm is a key success factor, however, being energized solely upon what you like or think is best for your customer is a recipe for lost Sales. A smart Salesperson allows the customer to express what he or she is interested in and then, and only then, should you express your recommendation.

Imagine a customer who is greeted by a Salesperson who is energetic, enthusiastic and enjoyable to be around. However, in this case, the Salesperson believes that the customer needs a product or service he or she is excited about or, for that matter, earns a higher commission. The customer, at first, may be enthused about the product or service but, is likely to soon realize that the suggestion is not for them. In this case, the Salesperson has wasted the customer's valuable time, or worse, the customer has run out of time and, therefore, has to leave. Either way, the Salesperson has lost a valuable opportunity.

Having interviewed thousands of applicants for a position in Sales, I often like to see how they would communicate information to a customer once they were hired. After handing them a product brochure and allowing them sufficient time to become familiar, I usually ask them to give me three reasons why I should purchase that particular product if I were an actual customer.

The responses I get are quite interesting. Whether the applicant has Sales experience or not, the applicant tends to ramble on about a particular feature that impressed them. Talking in circles makes it difficult to digest information, even when delivered enthusiastically. When they have finished and out of breath, I'm usually overwhelmed by the sheer amount of information they've unloaded and immediately have a hard time remembering everything they said.

Obviously, they had not learned 'The Power of 3'.

Imagine, going to a restaurant and asking the waiter to reveal the special for the day. To his delight he smiles and with great enthusiasm charges into a spill about the special, simmering New York Steak. Listening, your hunger agrees with the suggestion and he asks if you would like a sample. Of course, you say. In a few short minutes, he brings out a large flank of steak cooked to perfection and slices off an enormous piece and with fork in hand he tells you to open wide. You obey as the aroma is appealing. As the waiter pulls the fork away, leaving the piece of steak to your anxious pallet, you quickly realize that the piece of steak is larger than the circumference of your mouth. Struggling to chew and noticing the name on the menu, you soon realize the reason you came to this particular restaurant in the first place.

Antonio's, known for its great Italian cuisine.

Remember, The Law of Attraction does not allow room for continuous error. Doors of opportunity can and will open to you, however, walking through only to step into a hole is self-defeating. Therefore, talking your way out of a sale due to information overload negates any progress The Law of Attraction will give to you.

Understanding how a customer digests information is a key factor in successful selling.

So, how can you provide the right amount of information to satisfy the customer? What methodology can you use to avoid overwhelming the customer with too much information? If your product or service were water, for example, some customers have a need for information the size of a small tea cup and only want a very small amount of information. Other customers need information the size of a 55 gallon drum. The challenge that Salespeople face is determining the correct amount of content each and every customer is willing to accept.

'The Power of 3' is the answer.

This Sales methodology stems from the fact that most people can mentally manage three points of interest at one time. Three is easy to handle and allows the customer to choose which of the three interests them the most.

Imagine a restaurant where the waiter comes to the table with small samples of three specials. Briefly, he explains each item. Offering a sampling fork, he invites you to taste each of the three specials. Two of the three look delicious and the third appears to be something out of a science fiction novel.

No interest there. Of the two, one is completely delightful.

Your pallet screams for more and without hesitation, you order the special and later leave the restaurant telling all your friends about the experience.

Conveying information to a customer works in the same manner. People like choices and the mere fact that you are offering them three choices is empowering. It also gives the customer the feeling that they are in control. And, with choices, are they not in control?

Now, that we have a better understanding of 'The Power of 3', how is it used?

First, put yourself in a selling situation that you would actually find yourself. Standing alongside a customer in a retail store, in a conference room making a Sales presentation or third, a telephone Sales call. Now, as you introduce the product or service, you would start the conversation this way;

"The reason this product or service has become so popular is really a matter of three features, 1, 2 and 3. Which one would you be most interested in?"

Let the customer answer and then focus their attention on the benefits of that particular feature.

Ask questions. Learn why the customer is only interested in one particular feature. You can then begin to understand what will motivate the customer to buy.

This Sales methodology works best with most every customer you will encounter due to information overload. People have a lot on their plate. It is ludicrous to think that right before meeting the customer they had just finished a weekend retreat where relaxation and meditation was included to completely clear their mind. It's very likely the opposite! Your customer and their spouse might have been arguing in the car right before they walked in or they are experiencing stress from a situation completely unrelated to this particular buying decision.

'The Power of 3' respects the customer. It makes it easier for you to communicate only what the customer is interested in. It also conveys to the customer that you are not the typical talkative Salesperson that rambles on and on. When the customer tells you, "Well, actually, we're interested in the last one, in fact, that's the only reason we decided to look in the first place", it empowers the customer and brings them to your side of the table.

Learn to effectively use this Sales method and celebrate the results. Make it your aim to convey information in a way that is more easily understood. Avoid steering the customer over to features that only you are enthusiastic about or receive a higher commission.

Find out what the customer really needs and, most importantly, *wants*. Don't assume anything.

Always respect the customer's individuality. Ask questions and listen.

Really listen.

Then and only then will you achieve the degree of success in Sales using The Law of Attraction.

Emotion drives the sale

Fourteen
Emotional Payoffs

When customers look for a product or service, The Law of Attraction is at work. The image the customer visualizes in their mind of the product or service they are seeking starts a chain reaction that will lead them to you or you to them. When you share the benefits of what you are offering to them, you are, in fact, opening doors of opportunity to them. Subsequently, your responsibility is to lead them through one or more of these doors.

The door your customer eventually chooses to walk through will be determined by the emotional payoff your customer is seeking. The emotional payoff that customers subconsciously seek is more valuable to them than the price they pay to acquire your product or service. Here's a short list of emotional payoffs; Status, Safety, Security, Performance, Economy, Fear of Loss, and now more than ever, the Environment and Good Health.

Think Hybrid and All Natural.

Customers today seek out to satisfy these human emotions with most every form of product or service they purchase.

So, let's look at a few examples to see the role that human emotions play and how *The Power of Recognition* can deliver them.

First, let's examine *Valet Parking*. Not too long ago, I sat outside an Italian restaurant waiting for a business associate. I was a little early for dinner so, I took the time to watch other customers coming into the restaurant. If only I had a camera. It was an exhibition of human emotion at work.

As I watched the first customer drive up in a new automobile to valet park, I looked over at where I had parked my car. It's not the fact that I was too cheap to park valet style but, there were only two cars parked in the regular parking area and it was not even forty feet away from the entrance. Unless someone had a physical impairment of some kind at that moment, there really wasn't any valid reason to valet park.

As I watched each customer step out of their automobile to valet park, not once did I see anyone with any type of physical impairment. Not one person used a cane, a walker, a wheel chair or stepped out of their vehicle with a peg leg requiring valet parking. Now, I'm not a doctor, but, everyone appeared to be in excellent physical condition.

Sitting there, outside the restaurant for those few minutes, there must have been a total of four customers who parked, valet style. After the last customer went inside, I looked back at the regular parking area and noticed that one more car was sitting there next to mine. That was absolutely amazing, I thought. And, only a short forty feet away from the front door of the restaurant. Not, a walk up Mount Everest.

It was then that I had more of an appreciation for the human emotion we know as *Status*.

Each one of the four stepping out of their automobile was not only in good physical health but, their chest was pushed out and their chin was up. Having the opportunity to drive up, hand your keys to someone dressed in a uniform to park your car for you is an example of the human emotion, *Status*.

This human emotion is very powerful and the employee in uniform who took the keys delivered it along with *The Power of Recognition*.

Another human emotion *Safety and Security* is at work in many products and services.

Sometimes these two human emotions are referred to as *Peace of Mind*. Therefore, just about any product or service, if pointed out by the Salesperson, can deliver this strong human emotion.

Last year, I had a conversation with a Salesperson who sells new cars. We were discussing the subject of how to overcome price when dealing with a customer. The Salesperson then related how an elderly woman and her daughter came in to look for a new car. The Salesperson explained that the woman, much to his surprise was more interested in the headlights than any of the new features the vehicle offered. He said she wasn't that interested in the new air conditioned seats, the updated ten speaker stereo system or the new vehicle warranty or even the current rebate being offered.

He said she wanted to come back after dark with her husband and for him to see for himself how much better the Halogen Headlights were over their present vehicle.

Arriving after dark, the Salesperson gave the keys to the new vehicle to the husband so that he could experience the new headlights. Upon their arrival back to the dealership, he took the couple inside. Sitting at his desk, the Salesperson said he had barely started the paperwork in order to present a price to the couple when the woman, totally by surprise, pulled out her checkbook and asked the Salesperson, "how much do I write the check for".

The Salesperson related that he could not believe how this woman could be so ready to buy and not show the least bit of concern about price when most customers, according to him, "want to argue, fight and haggle over price". I asked him what lesson had he learned from the experience with this elderly couple. He said that some customers aren't that concerned about price. He added that he would like to have more customers just like them as his job would be that much easier and certainly more profitable. I told him I agreed but, asked him again what lesson had he learned. He said that he really hadn't given it that much thought.

Then I asked why he thought the customer was more interested in the headlights than the ten speaker stereo system or the updated warranty or even the rebate.

He said, in his first conversation with her when the daughter was present that she was worried about her husband driving at night. He was in his early seventies and his eyesight was not what it used to be. She not only worried about him driving alone at night but, there had been a few close calls when he was behind the wheel driving home late at night and she was in the front passenger seat. She tried but, couldn't control what hours he drove as he was determined not to have anyone drive for him. I asked the Salesperson to describe the elderly woman at that moment when she shared her personal concerns about her husband. What he said next came as no surprise. "She looked more than a little worried."

Although anyone in Sales reading this may say that this particular example is an extreme case. I beg to differ. Each and every day, customers seek out products and services that satisfy one or more human emotion. In many cases, as easily seen in this one with the elderly couple, the Salesperson completely missed two human emotions, *Safety and Security*.

Remember, price is less of an issue when the customer sees value in the product or service and especially when the customer wants the product or service *more* than the Salesperson wants the sale. This phenomenon occurs when the customer's emotional need or payoff is satisfied.

How can you help the customer to want the product more than you desire the sale? The answer is to listen, really listen to what your customer is asking. Most questions that are asked by a customer will lead to one or more emotional payoffs. Too many times, a Salesperson is excited about what's new this year or is so excited about what he or she likes about a product or service that the customer's wants and needs are completely overlooked. Let's review the case of the elderly couple just to make sure we haven't missed the 'how to' of this example. We know the Salesperson missed recognizing that *Safety and Security* was the human emotion the woman was seeking. The question is; at what moment should he have recognized it even without the customer disclosing her concerns about her husband's failing eyesight?

The answer lies in observing her behavior when he explained the vehicle's key features or when she started asking questions. Observing a customer's behavior when presenting a product or service is the where you can best determine the customer's emotional payoff.

Usually, it is what the customer is trying to say rather than what they are actually saying that leads you to identify the correct payoff that the customer is trying to achieve.

It's Not The Feature They're After

Customers choose a product or service that will make them feel a certain way. Focusing on features alone will limit your ability to close the sale.

When talking to the customer, try to identify what emotional payoff they are trying to satisfy. Listen to the questions they pose.

Where is the customer coming from?

What are they really after?

Understanding that human emotion plays an important role with every customer buying decision will help you to determine what will motivate the customer to purchase your product or service, regardless of price.

*Ask not what your customer can do for you,
rather ask what you can do for your customer*

Fifteen
The Value of Questions

Imagine yourself hiking in one of America's national parks. You and your friends chose to spend the day making your way through one of the more popular hiking trails. Late in the day, one of your friends notices a graceful deer making its way through the park. Without hesitation, you leave the trail and follow the deer from a distance.

As the deer moves out of sight, you make your way back to the trail. As you walk back, the sun fades behind the nearest mountain leaving you and your friends to make your way in the dark. Looking for the trail, you search for a flashlight. Finding one in your back-pack, you let out a sigh of relief as the bright light from the end of the cylinder cuts through the darkness. With flashlight in hand, you're able to make out familiar landmarks that finally lead you back to the trail's end.

When a customer seeks a product or service, it can be difficult to identify what specific benefit the customer is trying to acquire. It can be equally difficult when the customer does not readily identify what they really want or need. Many times, customers say one thing and mean another or they may even change their mind.

Like the flashlight that eventually lead you and your friends back to the trail, asking your customer specific questions will shed light in the direction that will eventually lead the customer to the purchase of your product or service.

Questions are to Salespeople as a guide dog is to the blind. You must learn how to effectively use questions to guide your customer through the Sales process.

As discussed in an earlier chapter, the 'Power of 3' is a powerful tool to showcase what you have to offer while helping to identify exactly what will motivate the customer to make the final purchase. Start by mentioning three distinct things that sets your product or service apart and then ask the customer which of those three would appeal to them the most. This will help to focus attention on what the customer is really interested in. If the customer is not interested in any of the three, in most cases it will cause the customer to reveal something else that will motivate them to buy.

Remember, just talking about the many features and benefits your product or service offers, in and of itself, will not motivate the customer to buy. Like a detective examining a crime scene, you must uncover clues that reveal motive.

Therefore, when a customer asks a question, never answer outright without understanding what is driving or motivating the question. Try to determine the customer's degree of interest by answering their question *with* a question.

Here is an example. Let's imagine the customer has asked whether the product was available in the color blue. You could answer yes it is or no it is not. Either way you've answered, you haven't gained any additional information from the customer that would help you close the sale.

Remember, *knowledge is power.* You must gain as much information from the customer as you possibly can. Therefore, you would answer the customer's question with a question, such as, are you more interested in blue than any other color or, would you prefer blue? With your question, the customer may say, "yes, blue is the only color that I really want" or, "well, I prefer blue but, white or red will do just fine".

Without asking questions, you cannot determine what will motivate the customer's buying decision.

Asking Questions To Get More Information

I remember a number of years ago presenting a product to a customer who was much older than I was at the time. The customer never smiled or displayed any emotion and only listened as I presented my product. After a few minutes, the customer asked if the product I was selling had a specific ingredient. As I looked at the expression on his face, I assumed he wasn't too impressed with that particular ingredient. I knew the product I was selling did, in fact, contain that particular ingredient.

The customer had put me in an uncomfortable position. Do I dance around the question? Do I say that the product does not contain that particular ingredient when I knew full well that it did? Allowing only two or three seconds to go by and looking into his eyes, I decided to answer his question with a question of my own. "Are you familiar with that ingredient?", I asked. His answer really surprised me. I did not expect the customer to express a favorable opinion about the ingredient that he had asked about as his facial expression wasn't positive when he initially asked the question. After I had answered his question with a question, he said that he had read a great deal about the ingredient, was impressed by it and was very interested in knowing whether or not my product contained that particular ingredient.

I learned a valuable lesson that day.

Never assume what the customer is thinking. Ask questions to determine with more certainty what is on the customer's mind. Ask questions to understand what specifically is motivating the customer's buying decision.

Answering Price or Payment Questions

Questions are designed to gather information from the customer and to help move the sale forward. For example, if the customer were to ask you about the kind of payment they might have to pay, it would be best to learn more before answering. You might ask, what kind of payment were you hoping for?

The word 'hoping' is a valuable word in Sales. In fact, there are few words in the English language that are more important in Sales.

What is so special about this one little word?

The word, 'hoping', helps to manage the customer's expectations. Here is an example. Let's say you used wanting, needing, expecting or looking for. Could those words also be used? Let's find out. This is how those words actually sound;

What kind of payment do you want?

What kind of payment do you need?

What kind of payment were you expecting?

What kind of payment were you looking for?

These four examples appear to work but, they are not the correct choice as each one sets the customer's expectations too high. Once the customer answers with an amount using the words 'want, need, expecting or looking for', you are now obligated to make their desired payment a reality. Why? Because the way your question was phrased created the perception that you had a degree of authority over the amount of the payment.

In most cases, you will not have the power or authority to make their dream payment come true. If you do not have any degree of authority or control over their payment amount then, it would be wise not to create that impression in the first place. The word 'hoping', on the other hand, helps to manage the customer's expectations. Therefore, the customer is likely to give you a number but, they know that the desired payment may or may not happen.

Now, you are in a much safer position. You did not promise a payment that you could not deliver. When a customer brings up the subject of payment, it's usually premature for a Salesperson to speculate.

What if the Salesperson said the payment would likely be $400 to $500 dollars when the customer is thinking $300? Smart Salespeople use the right words when answering questions.

What kind of payment were you *hoping* for? With more information, the Salesperson can direct the customer to the right product or service that would fit within their budget.

In fact, after the customer states the amount of payment that they were hoping for, the Salesperson can move the sale along by simply stating, "I know the company has many lenders that would love to earn your business and I know our Manager will work hard to find a payment that will fit within your budget."

With this Sales strategy, the Salesperson is able to avoid stating a payment amount that would discourage the customer from continuing to shop.

By obtaining more information from the customer, you can successfully guide them to the right product or service and, more importantly, allow you the time and opportunity to justify the cost of the product or service they are interested in. This process is called, building value.

Building value means helping the customer to establish a frame of reference. Here's an example.

If the price is listed, the customer may suffer from sticker shock.

What is sticker shock?

Many Salespeople understand 'sticker shock' to mean that the customer thinks that the price is too high. This is a common behavior with customers and a very fundamental aspect of Sales. When a customer suffers from sticker shock it means that the customer has no *frame of reference*. In other words, they do not have enough information to agree or even disagree with the price.

Here's an example. Let's imagine that you noticed the watch I was wearing and you made a favorable comment.

Now, at this point you have no idea what it costs or perhaps you don't even know the brand. We can assume that you have no frame of reference when I tell you the price.

"Thank you. I wanted one of these for a long time. When I first saw it, I wasn't even looking for an expensive watch."

"Oh, really? What did it cost?"

"Well, I didn't pay full price but, it retailed for more than $10,000."

"What? $10,000? You're kidding, right?"

"No, I'm not kidding. That's what it would have cost if I had paid full retail for a Rolex."

"Oh, a Rolex! That's different."

You see, with no frame of reference, a customer has nothing to push against. The more the brand is established, the more the frame of reference the customer is likely to already have. As a Salesperson, you must build value in your product or service.

It's your responsibility to build value in what you're selling in order to justify the price in the customer's mind.

Many Salespeople complain about having to deal with the issue of price.

Dealing with price is less difficult when the Salesperson spends the necessary time to build value in the product or service offered.

Without understanding exactly what they are being asked to pay for, any normal customer will question the price or seek a lower price.

Asking questions gives you more time and opportunity to build value and, more importantly, enables the customer to justify the purchase price.

Asking Double Alternate Questions

Asking questions is one of the primary tools that a Salesperson has in his or her tool box.

Questions allow you to identify what is most likely to motivate the customer to buy. Questions also help you to lead the customer directly to the close.

Like road signs that lead to your destination, the right question at the right time will lead your customer to the final purchase of your product or service. Now, imagine you are traveling down a particular road headed to a specific destination. Would you intentionally take a left or right turn that would cause you to head in the opposite direction? Of, course not.

Unfortunately, Salespeople make this mistake without even realizing it. How?

By asking the customer a question that generates a negative response, which then moves the customer away from the final purchase. Here's an example of a question that can easily create a negative response.

Are you folks here to take advantage of our big sale?

Questions like these are perceived to be too forward and rarely work to your advantage.

Here is where the Double Alternate Question is invaluable. This type of question is an "either–or" question and helps you to move the customer to the final purchase.

Let's go back to the first question. Are you folks here to take advantage of our big sale? Could that question be changed to a Double Alternate Question? Yes. Simply by adding an appropriate alternate, such as;

"Are you folks here to take advantage of our promotion or to just browse our large inventory?"

You see, by adding the alternate, you removed the forcefulness and gave the customer room to specify their purpose for stopping in. Remember, with your questions, you should seek to *encourage* the customer and never discourage. Notice that the previous Double Alternate question encouraged the customer to shop whereas, the earlier question, "are you folks here to take advantage of our big sale", could easily discourage the customer.

The Double Alternate also allows you the opportunity to identify how close the customer is to being ready to buy. Here is where The Double Alternate becomes a test close.

"So, John, would you want our home delivery or would you prefer customer pick-up?" When the customer chooses one or the other, they are most likely ready to buy.

A Salesperson using The Double Alternate question throughout the entire Sales process can effectively close the customer without ever having to over-talk the sale.

Like road signs that eventually lead you to your final destination, the double alternate question should be used whenever possible to lead the customer to the final purchase.

More Than Information Alone

Asking questions will certainly help you to identify exactly what the customer is ultimately seeking in a particular product or service.

But, there's more. Asking your customer a series of questions helps you to be perceived by the customer as someone who is genuinely interested in assisting them to find what they are looking for. But, more important than being perceived as genuine is the act of true sincerity itself.

Questions create a sense of trustworthiness.

Your customer will perceive your questions as an earnest effort to satisfy their wants and needs. In other words, questions build trust.

When the customer feels that they can trust you, then asking them to buy when the time is right to close the sale will be much easier.

And, finally, remember that questions not only empower the customer, they also empower you.

Asking the right series of questions helps you to remain focused on the customer's ultimate decision to buy and what needs to happen for them to eventually purchase your product or service.

Assume and you will receive

Sixteen
Assume The Sale

Just about every Sales situation requires that the Salesperson assume the sale.

This is the Sales strategy that separates the professional Salesperson from the novice.

What does it mean to assume the sale?

The answer lies in uncovering the meaning of the word, assume. When you assume something, it means that you 'take as granted or true'.

A customer who calls to inquire about purchasing a product or stops in to look is a potential buyer who should be taken seriously.

A Salesperson, therefore, must assume that the customer will buy if the right product and the right price can be found.

You must take the position and assume that the customer will buy. Lacking assertiveness in this area will surely diminish your Sales volume.

A friend of mine who sells new roofs to homeowners explained how assuming the sale is necessary to get the customer to agree to a free written estimate.

He said that just handing the customer a card and inviting the customer to contact him directly when they were ready to purchase a new roof was not enough. Instead, he tells the customer that his company is providing free written estimates that particular day and also the next day. He then asks the customer this question; 'which day would be better for you?'

He went on to relate that assuming that the customer would need the written estimate, which of course they did, was the catalyst to get the ball rolling and eventually close the sale.

Many customers hate to make buying decisions. They will procrastinate and put off making a decision if the opportunity is afforded them.

Assuming the sale actually makes the decision to buy easier for the customer.

The customer is more comfortable with options rather than a direct question that calls for a decision on their part.

Get in the habit of crafting your questions in such a way that you assume the customer will buy when given the opportunity to do so.

With each and every customer, strive to assume each and every sale. You will find yourself closing more customers and, therefore, achieving your goals.

It Is A Mind-set

Taking an assumptive position is a mind-set that starts when you say hello to the customer.

When you first encounter the customer, make up your mind at that moment that the customer is going to buy.

You have, at your disposal, all the information they need to make a decision.

You have done the research and you know that the benefits of your product or service exceed the cost.

You truly must make up your mind that you are going to sell this customer. Having this form of mind-set creates success with your customer.

If they like you and feel that they can trust you, then you are very likely to make the sale.

*People accept and embrace change only
after they clearly see its benefit*

Seventeen
Monetize The Benefits

Money talks and is important to most every customer, as it should be. The term, monetize, means to 'coin into money'. When your product or service earns or saves the customer money, you should make that an important part of your Sales presentation.

As a Salesperson, the mistake can easily be made to take for granted that the customer sees what is obvious to you.

The monetary benefit.

Never assume that the customer immediately understands the monetary benefit of your product or service. In fact, you should never assume that the customer is automatically on the same page that you are. You should always put the benefits into proper perspective for them. Tell the customer clearly and distinctly what the monetary benefit of your product or service is.

Now, let's go one step further.

Years ago, during an experiment with a Sales presentation, which is extremely helpful and highly recommended, I decided to tell the customer that the product would save them enough money to take their spouse every month to the best restaurant in town for a year instead of the typical $5,000 savings every customer would eventually realize.

It worked!

I was amazed that the customer responded to free dinners at the best restaurant for a year rather than the $5,000 savings. Sometimes we cannot put our head around what a certain amount of money means in terms of the actual benefit. And, since that is often the case, putting the monetary benefit in simple to understand terms is what monetizing the benefit is, all about.

Now that you understand this principle, find a way to monetize the benefit of your product or service.

It does not always have to be money. You may find that the product or service saves the customer time. In that case, monetize the time. If your product or service saves the customer time, paint a mental picture of what the customer could do with that amount of extra time. Extra time for a round of golf, spend time at the beach, more time with family or, taking their spouse out to dinner, etc.

You will find that monetizing the benefit is fun for you and your customer. However, be warned that your customer may not be impressed with any amount of monetization.

What can you do then? If possible, find someone else in the company or organization that will appreciate, and more importantly, value the monetary benefit.

I remember talking some time ago to an experienced Salesperson about this very subject. He was selling a service to Doctors that reduced the amount of uncollected receivables from patients not covered by insurance.

He went on to relate how surprised he was that the majority of Doctors he spoke to did not respond to the amount of money he would help them to collect each and every year. He tried putting the amount of money into days, weeks and years but, with very little success. The Doctors just didn't seem to care.

What was the final solution? One day by coincidence, he spoke to the wife of one of the Doctors who also managed the office. He told her how much money he would help the Doctor to collect in receivables each year and then he went one step further. He monetized the benefit and told her that it would easily pay for a second home on the lake within a few short years.

He hit the jackpot as she was, at the time, trying to convince her husband to purchase a second home on a nearby lake resort.

When you help the customer to measure the benefits, you will be surprised at the results. By taking the extra step to monetize the benefit, you are actually personalizing the savings to the customer. You are making the benefit real and personal which is a major factor in successful selling.

Monetizing the benefits allows The Law of Attraction to work for your customer as they are able to visualize the actual benefits of your product or service.

Using this strategy at each and every customer encounter will improve your success and enable you to increase your total Sales volume.

Know when to speak

Eighteen
Stop Talking!

Every Salesperson endures, at one time or another, this all too common mistake - talking themselves out of a sale.

It is very understandable why this phenomenon happens when a Salesperson is new.

He or she is nervous and any gaps or silence is uncomfortable to the newbie and, therefore, the urge to fill the void with small talk takes place.

I cannot think of anything more self-destructing than over talking the sale.

How do you control the urge to keep talking when you should stop?

Is it just experience or self-discipline that suppresses any urge to keep on talking when it is obvious to the universe that the time to shut up has already passed?

Imagine a sponge that is completely dried out.

It hasn't tasted liquid of any kind for years.

Now, imagine taking that sponge and ever so carefully, submerging it into a large glass of water.

Next, pull the sponge back out and see how much water has actually soaked into the sponge.

Unless the sponge is the one on the tv commercial that can drink like an Egyptian camel, your sponge should be just as hard as the moment you let it taste water from the glass. You see, customers are very much like a hard sponge. They have been exposed to a significant amount of dry air or Sales and Marketing advertisements that causes their buying enthusiasm to dry up.

Customers today have become hardened to most every Sales pitch.

Most, if not all of your customers are much like the hard sponge and will resist the typical Sales pitch. That is why you must control the amount of words you use with a customer.

Measure Your Words

Every professional Salesperson measures their words. What does that mean? It simply means that you are selective with the type of words you use with a customer. It also means that a professional Salesperson measures or is fully cognizant of the amount or volume of words that he or she is using.

Measuring your words also means that you occasionally or even intentionally leave some of your words out. It is not so much as what you say on occasion as it is more of what you do not say that can make the difference with your customer.

A number of years ago, I was making a Sales presentation to the CEO of a large and well respected company.

He was pressing hard to get me to drop the price of our service below what I knew was profitable for our company. At that moment he made a comment that I completely ignored. I went ahead as if the words were never spoken.

The CEO was impressed that I had ignored his comment. He asked me how long I had been in Sales. I asked the ages of his children. I picked the child in the middle. The fact that I was able to move the subject off of price because of omitting certain words was invaluable and eventually led to the close.

Be Prepared

Every Salesperson has their ups and downs. Some days you are right on point with everything you say and do. You could turn rocks into gold and water into wine.

It all starts with the how you begin your day.

If you start the day off being late, forgetting an important Sales document, picking the wrong shirt or dress because you just didn't see the spaghetti stain then, the rest of the day is going to be a carbine copy.

This is The Law of Attraction. What you think about becomes your reality. The more you have consistent thoughts the more you receive the same reality.

Preparation is the best method of using The Law of Attraction to help you to get what you want. Being prepared means that events can and will fall into place as your positive and confident mind-set creates more of the same.

Start your preparation for the next day the night before. Even something as simple as having your clothes laid out or having the coffee pot ready can make a big difference with how the next day's activities will eventually turn out.

Selling is all about momentum and The Law of Attraction is propelled by the force of energy generated by what is going on inside your head.

This brings a whole new meaning to the expression;

Knowledge is Power.

Knowledge or, the confidence that preparation generates creates a powerful force that attracts others to you.

When you are aware that you are ready for the day, ready to meet your next Sales appointment and ready to tackle your next Sales call, then a positive momentum will be with you.

In any event, preparation is a powerful ally and should never be taken for granted. Make it your aim to be as prepared as you can. Strive to learn your competition's weaknesses and their strengths. Doing so will pay tremendous dividends and will allow The Law of Attraction to work to your continuous benefit.

Get The Signature!

Just as Salespeople have great days, other days are best forgotten. I recall one day where I absolutely blew the perfect sale or at least I thought I had.

I had made three contacts on a particular customer. The initial Sales call led the Manager to say that they were satisfied with the company they had already chosen. Next, the unexpected phone call from the same Manager as they were interested in an estimate as the other company could not provide their services in the required time frame and, the third contact where the Manager agreed to our services but, wanted to get the approval of the Owner.

The next contact is where I blew it. Absolutely and unequivocally shot myself in the proverbial foot.

The fourth contact amounted to a phone call less than ninety seconds from the time I left their office.

As I was driving to my next appointment, my cell phone rang. It was the Manager. He had talked to the Owner and they were ready to sign. He asked how far I had travelled from their office and could I quickly return? I must have had a momentary brain aneurism as my decision was foolish. I told the Manager that I had one stop to make and then I would gladly return. I was actually on a toll road and turning around would be a pain. I figured that I could make my next Sales call around the corner and then return as I would not have to reschedule the next appointment.

So, I told the Manager that I would be back in less than 2 hours. He agreed and so off I went to my next Sales call which turned out to be a waste of time.

Upon my return, the Owner of the company greeted me at the door and, instead of immediately obtaining a signature, which the Manager was eager to do 2 hours before, the Owner wanted to review my estimate again. Looking it over carefully, he said he needed to check on some of my figures and would get back to me. He did offer some words of comfort. He said that they were still likely to sign with us, but not before he personally had checked out the numbers on my estimate.

I left their office feeling completely and utterly foolish. I knew better. The extra delay had not been to my benefit. I reassured myself that the figures would stand and the only thing that I was losing was a few extra days waiting for their phone call telling me to come back and the Owner's admission that my figures were, indeed, accurate.

At least, that is what I told myself as I drove away.

The truth is that anything can and does happen in between. Therefore, when your customer agrees to the purchase of your product or service and is ready to sign and move forward then you must become an emergency vehicle responding to an accident. Inside your head, lights must be flashing. A loud and penetrating siren must be sounding. You must blast through an intersection after you feel that is safe to do so letting nothing stop you from getting the customer to sign once they have said, YES!

Do it NOW! This must be your mind-set. Do it now. Do it now.

Do It NOW!

After the customer says *yes*, the amount of time that elapses until they actually sign is dangerous and full of risk. Never count your chickens before they have hatched. You cannot start writing checks your paycheck will not cover.

Until you experience this event you will not *own* this critical step.

Human nature dictates that we must experience some events first-hand before we can fully appreciate the wisest course.

Our parents told us when we were three years old not to touch the hot stove. What did we do?

We touched the stove.

Experience is the best teacher when we are changed *by* the experience. Insanity is defined as doing the same thing over and over again expecting different results.

And, by the way, the Owner did call the next day and was ready to sign. I was glad as I knew full well that I had dodged another Sales killing bullet.

After it happens and you are bemoaning your mistake, come back and read this chapter again and let the words be indelibly inscribed into your memory vowing never to delay getting the signature again.

*The company you keep will
ultimately define you*

Nineteen
Pick Your Company

Interestingly enough, some individuals carelessly choose the company in which they keep. With about as much thought as someone choosing a fountain pen when scribbling notes while talking on the phone, in the same manner, these same individuals go about choosing their next employer.

This chapter deals with two types of company.

First is the employer or organization you have chosen to work for or be associated with.

Second are the co-workers you must associate with as well as the type of people you choose to spend time with away from work.

The Law of Attraction states that whatever you consistently focus on becomes your reality.

The people you work for, the employees you come in contact with and the people you spend time with all exert a degree of influence. Each and every one of them has an opinion on just about any subject matter imaginable. They have well established attitudes, values and standards of living that are deeply entrenched.

Like it or not, their attitudes, values and standards will rub off on you to some degree. Without making any conscious effort whatsoever, you will inevitably find yourself adopting some of the opinions and attitudes of these various influencers.

We like to think that we are our own man or woman and that we have absolute control over our own thinking. The reality, though, is quite different. While we do have a high degree of control over our own attitudes, values and standards, we are susceptible to the influence of others.

In 1974, the granddaughter of publishing magnate, William Randolph Hearst, and great-granddaughter of self-made millionaire George Hearst, gained notoriety when, after being kidnapped by the Symbionese Liberation Army (SLA), ultimately joined her captors in furthering their cause. Arrested after having taken part in a bank robbery with other SLA members, she was imprisoned for almost two years before her sentence was commuted by President Jimmy Carter. She was later granted a presidential pardon by President Bill Clinton in his last official act before leaving office.

The following is a true story and illustrates that others can have a dramatic influence on our attitudes, beliefs and values.

On February 4, 1974, the nineteen-year-old woman was taken from an apartment in Berkeley, California that she shared with her fiancé Steven Weed. She was kidnapped by a left-wing group called the Symbionese Liberation Army. When the attempt to swap Hearst for other SLA members failed, the SLA demanded that her family distribute $70 worth of food to each and every needy person in the state of California. This would require an amount estimated in the tens of millions of dollars. Responding, her father arranged for the immediate donation of $6 million worth of food to the poor in and around the California Bay Area. After the food distribution was made, the SLA refused to release the young woman because they said the food had been of poor quality.

In a tape recording that was later released to the press, the young woman stated that 'her father could have done better'.

On April 3, 1974, the woman announced on an audiotape that she had joined the SLA and assumed the name *Tania*.

On April 15, 1974, she was photographed holding an M1 while aiding in the robbery of the Sunset District branch of the Hibernia Bank in San Francisco. Using the name *Tania,* she asserted that she was committed to the goals of the SLA. She was later arrested in a San Francisco apartment with other SLA members. As she was being taken into custody, she listed her occupation as 'Urban Guerilla' and asked her defense attorney to report the following: "Tell everybody that I'm smiling, that I feel free and strong and I send my greetings and love to all the sisters and brothers out there".

During the trial, her attorney, F. Lee Bailey, claimed that she had been blindfolded, imprisoned in a narrow closet and physically and sexually abused. Her defense stated that her actions were the result of a successful brainwashing effort. Her defense attorney also argued that she had been coerced or intimidated into taking part in the robbery. However, the young woman refused to give any evidence against the other captured SLA members. Her actions were seen as complicity by the prosecution. She was convicted of bank robbery on March 20, 1976 and was sentenced to 35 years of imprisonment.

This example, while extreme, highlights a very important point that will impact your success using The Law of Attraction principles.

Her name was Patty Hearst and her experience underscores an enormous fact that many Salespeople overlook.

You are likely to adopt and become like the people you consistently associate with just as what you focus on consistently becomes your reality.

Every organization has its top Sales leaders as well as the bottom feeders.

If you are to benefit fully from The Law of Attraction, you must give serious consideration to the type of people you associate and spend time with whether at work or at play. They *will* influence your goals, dreams and desires to some degree.

Success in Sales using The Law of Attraction is futile if the people you spend time with are a poor influence. Eventually, their attitudes, lack of goals and poor life management will erode any progress you have made using The Law of Attraction principles.

Top Salespeople seek out and spend time with Sales Leaders even when the time spent with them is in the car listening to audio programs. You cannot and should not expect The Law of Attraction to be a Jeanie in a bottle.

Choose your association carefully

Just because you wish for something mean that your dream will become a reality.

Great effort on your part is required. However, it will be much easier to create your own future when you associate with other success minded Sales leaders.

Seek out and spend time with others who have similar goals and especially those who will encourage you to keep going in the quest for the realization of your hopes and dreams. Avoid individuals who are negative and discourage those who try reaching forward using The Law of Attraction.

Therefore, understanding that you are likely to be influenced by the people you spend the most time with should motivate you to carefully consider who you will associate with socially and as well as the workplace.

Equally important to your success using The Law of Attraction is the employer or organization that you ultimately choose to associate with.

This can be difficult if you are unemployed for an extended period of time and you find yourself interviewing with any employer who shows interest.

Unfortunately, the very worst time to be looking for employment is when you are out of a job. If you are currently employed and have a legitimate reason or motivation for leaving, then you should begin looking for a new employer now. Don't wait. Don't put off finding a new place of employment when you know deep down that your current job is not the best environment that will help you to advance.

In any case, be selective with respect to the employer or organization you will ultimately choose. If you sense that the ownership and the management of the company is not genuine or sincere and your intuition is telling you this painful truth then, by all means, listen to your inner voice and avoid the company altogether.

Take a serious approach when determining the management skills of any future employer or organization. You cannot obtain your goals and dreams all on your own. Your dominate thoughts can and will be influenced by others. At the very least, you will be distracted by those you spend consistent time with.

If you are interviewing for a new position, ask the interviewer who you will be spending the most amount of time with. At some point and, certainly prior to accepting the position, ask to meet that person. Ask to meet the supervisor. What is your first impression? Is this the type of person you aspire to imitate? Other than the technical aspects of the job, is this the person you want to model yourself after?

If the answer is no and you feel that you need to move on then, by all means, move on.

On the other hand, you may feel that due to finances that you must accept employment with a specific company even though it is not where you want to remain long term. If that is the case and, you do accept the position, do not become complacent or lazy in your search for the very best organization. Remember, the company you work for and those who are employed by that company will influence your attitudes and behaviors to some degree.

With respect to your employer and the people you will be associating with at work, you must expect some distraction in following The Law of Attraction principles. Unfortunately, you will encounter those who are not followers of The Law of Attraction whether they know it or not.

To a degree, their attitudes, values and standards can be very damaging. Imagine a raging house fire and you run in to save someone who is still trapped inside. Feeling that you have no choice, you choose to go in to the try and save them. The flames are everywhere and you get burned pulling the person out. Your burns could be first, second or third degree. In any case, you have been damaged.

The company and the people you associate with can be likened to a house fire. As an employee and unless you are ill, you have no choice but to show up each and every work day or else lose the job.

When exposed to bad influences, damage to your attitudes, standards and values can be likened to a first, second or even a third degree burn. The scars will last a very long time.

Every company or organization, though, is not a raging house fire. Many companies are excellent choices that can help perpetuate your dreams and desires. Great organizations not only set a tone, they create a perpetual atmosphere that is conducive to following The Law of

Attraction. This does not happen by accident. Great organizations, large and small, provide a working environment enabling you to pursue your goals, dreams and desires.

Remember, the company you keep will ultimately define you.

Keeping this forever in mind will help you to connect the dots to help you to get what you want.

Never allow anything or anyone to keep you from your goals.

Make every effort to surround yourself with people of the highest character with their own personal quest for achievement and success and who appreciate and, more importantly, follow The Law of Attraction.

*Your reality is the
sum of your thoughts*

Twenty
Living The Law of Attraction

Talk is cheap. Saying that you will do something is easy. Actually doing it is another matter.

Everyone wants to be successful. Everyone wants to be happy. Achieving real success and happiness is a real challenge and, one that cannot be taken lightly.

What is the secret to living The Law of Attraction? How do you put all of these necessary steps into play?

The First Step

The chapters in this book are the starting point. However, there are necessary steps you should take to help make living The Law of Attraction easier.

First, *remove every bit of negativity* from your life as you possibly can. This means everything.

If you like watching the evening news, STOP watching it!

There is more bad news in those few minutes than what most of us need in an entire year. Watching the evening news cannot and will not give you a positive outlook. If it is news that you want, use the internet where you can filter out the negativity.

If you cannot control it, why let it enter your mind?

Anxiety comes from things you cannot control. If you watch television or news programs that are negative, you are interrupting the positive flow from The Law of Attraction. You know that you cannot control what you see on television. Because you cannot control the outcome, feelings of anxiety are negative. Therefore, remove it. This does not mean that you should become insensitive to the suffering in the world, on the contrary, work to make the small world that you live in a better place.

If you have co-workers, neighbors, relatives or even friends who are consistently negative, cease altogether or limit the amount of time you spend with them. Their negativity is how they have learned to deal with their inadequacies, their faults, their imperfections and life's utter disappointments. Every minute that you spend with negative vibes robs you of your momentum with respect to The Law of Attraction.

Like attracts like and negativity breeds more negativity. Get away from these individuals fast or, at the very least, curtail your association with them to an absolute minimum. They are single-handedly stealing your potential for real success.

The Second Step

The second step is to *give back*. Just because you choose to skip the evening news, does not mean that you do not care about your fellow man. On the contrary, give back anyway you can.

This is certainly something that you can control.

Give back to society. Whether that means giving to charity or helping a friend or a neighbor in need is completely up to you. Giving of your time and resources to others will come back to you ten-fold.

Success alone will never make you happy. The number of zeros in your bank account will not, in and of itself, bring you the success and happiness that you are seeking. Success and wealth will, however, empower you and enable you to help others. Those who stand on the street corner begging for money are usually not in a position or frame of mind to help others. On the other hand, giving to others makes us feel better about ourselves.

Each month, try to help someone. Stay alert to anyone who may need your help. This does not mean necessarily those in need of money. You can easily find individuals belonging to that group. When sitting at your next stop light, just look over and observe the homeless who are obviously in need of help. If you choose to hand over a few dollars then, you are certainly giving back. But, that is not the point here.

Handing someone a dollar versus helping someone to continually benefit themselves brings lasting satisfaction, to you and to them.

What if you cannot find anyone to help? That does happen. We can easily live in a cocoon where we just do not meet people who are either needing help or wanting it.

In that case, join a group. There are many networking groups in every field. Join them so as not to take from them but, to give back. If you are alert, you will easily find someone in the group who is eager to accept your help. That will give you more satisfaction and pleasure than any amount of money you could ever acquire.

The Third Step

The third step in living The Law of Attraction is that of understanding why 90% of people fail. And, what is it? It is a lack of basic *interpersonal communication skills* that hinders even the most talented people.

Many years ago, The Carnegie Institute of Technology analyzed the records of some 10,000 people. After an exhaustive amount of research, they discovered that 15% of success was a result of technical training, intelligence and skill on the job and 85% of success was due to personality and more specifically, the person's ability to deal with others successfully.

Interestingly, the Bureau of Vocational Guidance at Harvard University conducted a study of thousands of people who had earlier been fired. They found that for every one person who lost their job as a result of failure to do the work, two lost their job as a result of a failure to deal with others successfully.

Those who are likely to become successful are not the ones with the most brains or even the highest set of technical skills. In most all cases, those who are the most successful are those who can successfully get along with other people. With the increased amount of technology used in business today, one would think that increasing ones technical knowledge would give the advantage.

While technical knowledge is important, dealing with people is even more important to your success.

The Fourth Step

The fourth step is to *never take yourself too seriously*. Yes, taking yourself a little less serious means that you are modest in your dealings with other people.

Modesty means knowing your limitations. It is the opposite of arrogance. A modest person listens to helpful criticism.

This is not to be confused with Step One, running away from negative friends. Negativity can and will interrupt The Law of Attraction because it focuses on what you do not want. However, there is a difference in being negative and helpful criticism.

When someone gives you a suggestion, do you listen? How do you react? Most become defensive when it comes to receiving criticism. That is human nature, plain and simple. But, a wise person listens to suggestions. When you are seeking advice or feedback, ask one of these questions, "How could I improve on this?" or "What would you do to make it better?"

This approach allows the other person to understand that you are open to suggestions. And, they are more likely to give you a straightforward and honest opinion without hurting your feelings. Seeking advice is always the wise choice. Continue to stay alert to anyone and everyone who is interested in your success.

Pay close attention to those who are a proponent of The Law of Attraction. They understand this mighty law and appreciate its timeless principles.

The Fifth Step

The fifth step is to be *less judgmental* in how you assess others. Everyone has their own personal standards and values.

We all have our own personal and individual filters and we judge others and certain circumstances by our previous life experiences. What is important to us may not be important to someone else.

Our being less judgmental means that we do not impose our standards on others. When we appreciate that other people see things differently, we will find that our lives are less complicated and less difficult.

Do not forever demand that others agree with your point of view. Try instead to understand theirs.

If you attempt to see things from others perspective, you will learn how to sell them on your product or service. You will understand where they are coming from as you learn their point of view. This is a key element in living The Law of Attraction.

You cannot get what you want without the permission and assistance from others.

In Sales, it will either be your customer or your employer.

Therefore, do not demand that those you communicate with always see it your way. They have their own challenges and, more importantly, their own selfish motivations.

They may not agree to accept your product or service for reasons that do not make any reasonable sense. To you, the obvious is right in front of them. You have explained the features and benefits and, in your lofty opinion, a blind person would not stumble over this crystal clear opportunity. Even so, your customer may continue to give you reasons or excuses that make absolutely no sense, whatsoever. However, forcing the issue can leave you empty handed.

It is your responsibility to identify why they are giving you this particular excuse. The answer to your challenge is the fact that they have not revealed their true motivation and it is up to you to find out what it is and how you can overcome it.

Just remember. Every single customer is like a different country on the world map, so to speak. They have their own history of experience or have no personal experience with your product or service. They have their own culture, which can be defined as likes and dislikes. They have their own language with respect to how they communicate their wants and needs.

And, they have their own set of challenges to overcome.

Therefore, treating every customer the same by trying to fit each one into your set of standards can and will make your career in Sales extremely difficult. Instead, make every effort to understand your customer's point of view and what is or is not important to them. Only then will you benefit from The Law of Attraction.

The Sixth Step

The sixth step for living The Law of Attraction has to do with *appreciating others for who they are* and not for what they will do for you.

This human flaw presents itself when recognizing and appreciating someone only for what they can do for us. Do we not realize how transparent this is? Can we not see how easily this type of behavior is detected by those we direct it to?

Obviously not, as this is a prevailing trait for many. We have seen it many times. Someone we meet is not that interested in us until they find out we can benefit them in some way. This human flaw is counterproductive to The Law of Attraction.

For the law to work in our behalf, we must continually send out messages that are positive and not negative. When we only want to use others for their benefit to us, we break The Law of Attraction frequency.

Attracting positive outcomes, in most all cases, involves attracting other people to you. Getting to the top, if you will, does not mean that you walked or ran to the top by yourself, it involves the assistance from others who help you get to the top.

The Seventh Step

The seventh step is *setting the stage*. In each and every encounter with customers, you have the opportunity to set the stage.

For example, if you were a door-to-door Salesperson, you set the stage when you say, "I'm sorry to bother you, but…". Here, you have set the stage to remain defensive for the rest of your presentation. This Salesperson will be defending anything and everything, including the price and whether or not the right time to buy is now or later.

Setting the stage involves letting the customer know immediately what you have and how they will benefit from your product or service. If you are interrupting their day, they already know it. No need to focus attention on the obvious. Instead, get to the point about the reason for your interruption.

As soon as the customer can visualize the benefit of your product or service, the fact that you have interrupted them is quickly forgotten.

Instead, you might use this approach. "Hello, we're finding that homeowners are having trouble with this particular issue, I'm stopping by to share information that our customers have found to be a solution".

Here, you immediately highlighted the crisis or problem. Then, you explained that there is a solution and you are making yourself available to them to join your list of satisfied customers.

Setting the stage will aid you in that it communicates to your customer what you expect of them. The fact that you remain positive in your approach is no coincidence. The Law of Attraction can and will guide you to customers who are seeking out a solution to their problems.

The Eighth Step

This step involves *avoiding the habit of being critical* of others as there are rare circumstances that truly justify harsh criticism. Being critical creates a negative environment that conflicts with the principals of The Law of Attraction.

This type of behavior never accomplishes your goal of achieving success. It is always counterproductive and creates a communication barrier that can be extremely harmful to both you and the other person.

There are many examples that illustrate the patience of the 16th President and his understanding of human nature and the mistakes and flaws of others.

Abraham Lincoln rarely criticized his subordinates. He was known for taking out his frustrations by writing the offender a letter and then never actually sending it.

On one noteworthy occasion, Lincoln sat in the parlor for more than an hour waiting on General George McClellan to arrive home. Upon entering, the General went upstairs without saying a word. Finally, a message was sent to the waiting President stating that the General had retired.

Most of us would have become angry beyond words. Our anger would have likely to have resulted in the firing of the General.

While the President never again attempted to meet General McClellan at his home and arranged all future meetings at the White House, Lincoln never voiced his disappointment.

He let it go.

The core reason people criticize others harshly is the fact that they are usually unhappy with themselves and the painful truth of their unhappiness spills over to those they choose to find fault. Likewise, when an individual puts someone else down, it is usually done in an effort to elevate themselves. To make themselves feel better.

Very few successful people use verbal criticism.

In his book, 'How To Win Friends & Influence People', Dale Carnegie relates the story of Charles Schwab. One day, Mr. Schwab was entering his steel mill and noticed a few employees smoking right under a sign that demanded otherwise.

Instead of harshly criticizing his employees, the wise business owner knew just how to reprimand the offenders and leave their pride and dignity intact. Charles Schwab walked over to the small group of employees, pulled out cigars and while handing them to each employee, said *"I'll appreciate it boys, if you would smoke these on the outside"*. The wise man knew that his employees were valuable to him and his company. He knew that to criticize an employee, especially in front of others, was a tragic mistake.

Living The Law Attraction literally means that you need and will continue to need the continued support of others. Learning how to communicate effectively, especially when it comes to criticism, is a large factor in your ultimate success.

The Ninth Step

The ninth step is the exact opposite of number eight. Living The Law of Attraction involves exhibiting *enthusiasm*. Remember, if you are focused on your goal, you will attract what you continually think about.

Enthusiasm is the fuel that will enable you and empower you to stay focused and positive as you continue to pursue your goals and dreams. Demonstrating enthusiasm consistently is challenging as life brings us its ups and downs.

So, how can you remain enthusiastic when it appears that there isn't anything at present to be enthusiastic about?

To be enthusiastic, you need information.

Digging for more information is the catalyst for increased energy and enthusiasm when presenting your product or service.

Remember back when you first became enthusiastic about your product or service. Your enthusiasm was a result of something you learned or perhaps even stumbled upon. I remember a time when I became enthusiastic about a product I had already been selling for quite a while. I had it available to customers but, there was no "Wow" factor with this particular product. Then one day a customer asked me a question about this particular product. I didn't have an answer right away so I told the customer I would find out before the end of the day and get back. And, that's what I did. I checked with a supplier and found out that our product had something few other competitors had. With this knowledge, my enthusiasm empowered me to focus on that product for an entire month and my entire Sales grew by more than 50%.

Enthusiasm comes from information. Whether you become enthusiastic because of what your product or service will do or how much it will help others does not matter. Yes, the key to enthusiasm is knowledge. Therefore, continually look for information, trends and changes in your industry that reveals a new opportunity to expand your Sales or your customer base. If you do, you will remain on the cutting edge of success and will experience firsthand the power of The Law of Attraction.

The Tenth Step

The tenth and most important step for living the Law of Attraction is *the size of your thinking*. In other words, the size of your goals determines the outcome.

If you think small, you receive small. This does not mean that you should become greedy or selfish. On the contrary, it means that the size of your thinking determines the size and the amount you will attract.

For example, if you only dream of a one bedroom apartment then that is precisely what you will receive, a one bedroom apartment. However, if a one bedroom apartment is perfect for your personal needs, then the size of your thinking is correct. On the other hand, if you visualize and focus on a home with three bedrooms, then The Law of Attraction will help you acquire a three bedroom house.

Remember, the size of your thinking determines what you will receive as a result of The Law of Attraction. The primary reason few people get what they want is the ultimate truth that they do not believe that getting what they want could ever become a reality. And, as such, their thinking becomes a self-fulfilled prophecy. They never get what they really want.

In his masterful book, *The Magic of Thinking Big*, David Schwartz makes an important point. He said, "The tendency for so many people to think small means there is much less competition than you think for a rewarding career". He makes a valid point. Most Salespeople do think small. They think that they could never land that large account and so they never try.

This presents a tremendous opportunity to the Salesperson who does think big. It does not mean that he or she throws caution to the wind and makes no sales calls on small companies. In many cases, it takes considerable time to land a larger account. But, you will find that there are fewer Salespeople calling on large accounts and the effort is rewarding when you do think big and invest some of your time in prospecting and landing these prized accounts.

In order for you to get what you really want, determine what it is that you really want. Don't make the mistake of limiting the size of what you want. Try to be reasonable without limiting yourself. In other words, if you said that in one year you would like to have an extra $10,000 in the bank, in your savings account or in your retirement account that is not an unrealistic goal for most of us.

Saying that we would like $10 million is another matter and probably unrealistic. Living The Law of Attraction everyday is a journey. It is filled with optimism and hope for the future. You have many talents and abilities, some of which you either are unaware of or downplay.

Every single person has talents. You have talents. The abilities you possess are talents that the rest of us only dream of.

Never let anyone tell you that you cannot accomplish your goals or dreams. History is filled with those who pushed forward and accomplished their goals and dreams while the negative crowd stood by, wagging their heads saying all along that it could never be done. Focus your attention instead on what your life will be like once you have reached your goal's destination.

What kind of house will you live in?

What kind of car do you want to drive?

What kind of schools will your children attend?

Where will you go on your next vacation?

Who are your true friends who want you to succeed?

Do they share the same positive outlook on life? These are a few of the many questions that life is shouting at you right now. Ignoring these and many other questions will go on creating the same world that you presently find yourself living in. However, addressing these questions and asking yourself, 'what do I really want out of life', is without a doubt, living The Law of Attraction.

Make it your aim only to use the past to create a better future for you and those you care deeply about.

Do not allow your past to rob you of the energy needed to move forward. Instead, use the past to help you create your own future.

The Law of Attraction is real.

Use what you have learned to keep fear from dictating the decisions you will face in the future. Maintain a positive mental attitude and be continually grateful for what you do have.

Be resolved to use every bit of knowledge you can acquire to help you to make your dreams a reality. And, finally, help anyone and everyone you can to learn and understand what we have come to know and fully appreciate, this mighty law,

The Law of Attraction!

Other Law of Attraction Titles Coming Soon

The Law of Attraction For …Starting Your Own Business

The Law of Attraction For …The Pursuit of Happiness

The Law of Attraction For …Landing Your Dream Job

The Law of Attraction For …Creating Wealth

The Law of Attraction For …Weight Loss

The Law of Attraction For …Public Speaking

The Law of Attraction For …Writers

The Law of Attraction For …Buying and Selling A Home

The Law of Attraction For …Investing

The Law of Attraction For …Actors

The Law of Attraction For …Creating Lasting Relationships

The Law of Attraction For …Marriage

The Law of Attraction For …Parents

The Law of Attraction For …Teenagers

The Law of Attraction For …Managing Your Life

The Law of Attraction For …Getting and Staying Fit

The Law of Attraction For …Personal Finance

Check InterSkillMedia.com For New Titles!

Procrastination Elimination by Susan Lynn Perry - Audio CD

Mother Cub – A Story of Autism – Audio CD

Divorce Without Going Broke – Audio CD

Kids How To Stay Safe - DVD

Body Language: Success & Confidence for Men - DVD

Body Language: Success & Confidence for Women - DVD

Body Language: Dating Cues for Men - DVD

Body Language: Dating Cues for Women - DVD

Body Language: Waiters How To Increase Your Tips - DVD

**For these Audio & Video titles,
visit: www.InterSkillMedia.com**

Employee Training Videos

Body Language: Hiring & Interviewing Employees – DVD
Body Language: Management - DVD
Body Language: Customer Service and Sales – DVD
Body Language: HealthCare Customer Service - DVD

**For these titles, please email;
Sales@interskillmedia.com**

**Copyright 2009 – InterSkillMedia
All Rights Reserved.**

www.ingramcontent.com/pod-product-compliance
Lightning Source LLC
LaVergne TN
LVHW041613070426
835507LV00008B/209